I0172512

Spectral Realms

No. 11 ‡ Summer 2019

Edited by S. T. Joshi

The spectral realms that thou canst see
With eyes veil'd from the world and me.

H. P. LOVECRAFT, "To a Dreamer"

SPECTRAL REALMS is published twice a year by Hippocampus Press,
P.O. Box 641, New York, NY 10156 (www.hippocampuspress.com).
Cover art and design by Daniel V. Sauer
Hippocampus Press logo by Anastasia Damianakos.

ISBN 978-1-61498-273-9   ISSN 2333-4215

Contents

To W. H. Pugmire
1951–2019
in memoriam

Poems

The Tomb of Wilum Hopfrog Pugmire

Wade German

In some strange hollow fearful minds defame,
The sentinels of Sesqua keep the path;
One reaches it through circles of black math
To find the obelisk that bears his name.

Here, in the hour twilight creatures dwell
The mossy mound that is their master's tomb,
The rosy shadows blend with purple gloom
And moan before the Night's black magic spell.

Even as he explores dark gulfs of sleep,
Weird spirits conjured out of unknown space,
Like lovely horrors, at his grave increase;

They hear the wisdom of the worms that creep;
And ever watchful, ward his resting place
From those who would profane his dreamful peace.

The Blackbird's Ghost

Abigail Wildes

Here in this room with ceiling high
Ghostly flutter 'bove where I lie
Small foul soul caught in between
This world here and the world unseen

Flitting 'round from arch to beam
Chirping out a little scream
A child's hands so long ago
Removed each feather, beak and toe

Boredom made the child callous
A Curiosity with unborn malice
But death was cruel to tiny beast
The torture long 'fore life decreased

So it now flies above my bed
Knows not how to be quite dead
Fallen feathers 'round the room
I replace each one, a mended plume

Healing up each little pain
Till creature is made whole again
Open the window and release!
May little soul now Rest In Peace.

Temptation Entombed

David Barker

Within the vault I found the tome I sought
Concealed behind the codex all must heed
By him who penned those words I yearned to read.
Though peril to my mortal soul they brought,
Hypnotic verses deep with evil fraught
Contrived to teach the weak The Devil's creed;
Then all of Hell's red demons would be freed—
Upon the Earth a savage fury wrought.

As tempted as I was this book to steal,
Some wiser inner voice commanded, "No!"
I dropped the tainted volume to the ground
And prayed the noise it made would not reveal
My presence in those dusty stacks below
To monks above alert for telltale sound.

Eternal Lovers

Carl E. Reed

Prologue:

We loved the grand old gilded books
that sang of romance in prose or rhyme;
twinned souls cleaving ever more together—
nevermore alone, till the end of time.

Verse:

An ember pops in the smoldering hearth—
spark of orange in empurpling dark;
I nurse a brandy in the wingback chair,
ensconced amongst books in my library lair,

Too weary to rise in the pregnant gloom;
the candles gone out, I know that soon
you will be with me once again—
my lover, my wife—an abominable sin.

& there—just now—in the dust-moted black—
a prickling tickle at the base of my neck:
a gentling hand, feather-soft & sweet;
moth-brushed lips that hungrily seek

my own as I groan & twist in the high
wingback chair in which you sighed
& moaned over tomes of romance fair—
your kindled eyes, your lustrous hair

once glinted here by hearth fire glow
until the day—alack! & woe!—
a lover's letter proved you whore,
& bereft I left you dead on the moor.

Covert

F. J. Bergmann

She always wore basic black, the better to blend
with their dark coats, the better to hide the stains.
They disdained informality. Gold lit up their eyes
and flared along their cheekbones as leaves fell

from a green inferno. Their speech, like their ears,
was clipped and to the point. She thought them
romantic as Hell, but never noticed that their replies
to her importunings consisted of long silences

and not meeting her eyes. Nor did she watch them
as closely as she ought. She saw only what she wished
to see in a garden of dark flowers, candelabra-lit.
She glowed with stolen moonlight, an illumination

that changed them only from wolf to dog, dog
to wolf. They manufactured their own shadows.

after *A Wolf in Wolf's Clothing*, Kelli Hoppman,
oil on board, 30" × 48", 2008

On a Threadbare Photograph of H.P.L. at 66 College St.

Manuel Pérez-Campos

As the tourmaline rhythms of the Milky
Way dwarf the spirit & the First Baptist
church campanile, you (a revenant in
an old-fashion'd suit whose art of
ventriloquizing the lucifugous festival
of infinity has been dreamt under
the auspices of Urania) stand steadfast
by your porch as if some ethereal extension
of Britannia & wonder, as your hunger
prospers, when is it that the night-gaunts
shall come again? O in your hazel eyes
I can hear you oppress'd by the thought
of voids beyond the sidewalk under your shoes
& beyond the clouds over your fedora.

The Witch of Hearts

Chelsea Arrington

The Witch of Hearts cares naught for jewels,
    Roses, wine, or verse.
The blood of men alone's what fuels,
    Loving hex or curse.

In bed, she hosts dark men, youths fair,
    Sailors, kings, and sheiks.
They travel far for this jew'l rare;
    Daring seas and lakes.

They lose their minds, their wit, and brains.
    Goddess, she is Queen;
'Twould treason be to quit their chains—
    One they cannot wean.

Her throne is wet with lovers' blood;
    Bodies strewn about.
Her lips engorged, a deepened rud.
    There's no room for doubt;

For on her tripods, glitt'ring red,
    Spy a sight so grim!
The hearts of men who've rut her bed,
    Lovely as a hymn.

Upon this feast, our witch laid waste:
  Belly full, content.
The hearts of men are to her taste.
  She'll not soon repent.

You cannot flee her siren's song;
  She will take your heart.
It isn't right, nor is it wrong:
  Loving is her art.

The Legend of Vlad and Juztina

(A Song for the Undead)

Tatiana Strange

Juztina: Listen my love. . . . Can you hear them wailing?
Do you not see their tortured souls wandering the halls?
The cries of the Dead creep into my chambers and haunt my dreams,
There, an endless valley of rotting corpses,
Our land is soaked with blood, our wells swell with tears of misery,
And I, am tangled in your lies, an impenetrable veil of deceit.

Vlad: You can see the hatred blackening my eyes,
The evil within seeps into all around me,
The blackness consumes all,
But my vengeance is justified!
This land reeks of blood but alas it is free.
When the blood drips from their flesh into my glass,
Those who watch will shudder and draw back,
Appalled as I dance on their graves and laugh.

Both: Songs are sung in the marketplace where the slaughtered hang
    for all to see,
Blood-chilling moans are carried on the wind,
The agony of the Damned, still screaming,
They will tell tales of the legend of our love,
The mystery of our ghastly legacy.

Juztina: I hear them walk the halls at night,

Their voices as hollow as the sound of their steps;
Their screams of torment are maddening!
The macabre songs of the Dead. . . .

Vlad: I fear you have drifted from me, my love . . .
There is such a strange look in your eyes,
There is no trace of you,
With bitterness in my heart and blood upon my lips,
I now kiss you good night.

A note on this work:
It was inspired by Vlad Tepes and the tragedy of his first romance. Historians
still cannot agree whether her name was Juztina or not. Very little is known
about her except that she died during the war of 1462 as the result of suicide. It
is assumed that he kept his atrocities hidden from her and that she only heard
rumors of them at the castle. This may have driven her mad.

A Lady and Her Monster

Christopher Collingwood

You married a monster
A rag doll of stapled flesh
The bastard son of science
A disjointed tapestry
Woven into admiration
Your beauty hung upon the wall
Smiling in affection
To all broken things
But you have always been that way
Freeing the moth, from the butterfly net
Sympathetic to a morbid deformity
I can see your husband sitting in a jar
Its face pressed against the glass
Jaw sticking through its cheek
That sad lonely look that drew you to it
Your neighbours chasing
A malformed innocent
Loathing the progeny of scholars
A clumsy lump of flesh, stumbling into your arms
Your sympathies held it to your breast
Nursing the pain of injustice
Your warmth soothing the true torment
You learnt its depth of feeling
A broken heart, beating behind a metal plate
Its eyes reaching

The pain you never knew
The truth of beauty
Is loneliness
Then you forgot the monster's face
And recognised your husband Walter
The home you built together
Discovering the true grief of man's creation
The knowledge of life without love.

The Hill of Bones

G. O. Clark

He stood upon
the hill of bones when
very young, his Mom
snapping photos.

He experienced
first love atop the hill
of bones, the thrill turning
brittle over time.

He held his ground
upon the hill of bones,
home but a postmark on
a distant shore.

They built their home
upon the hill of bones, good
days and bad passing, their
genes future bound.

They were buried side
by side upon the hill of bones;
two more epitaphs added to
all those come before.

Space-Time

Ron L. Johnson II

We are just a brief moment in the space-time continuum.
When we think of our beginning, do we project the past,
Reversing time with our thoughts?
And when we travel at the speed of thought,
Can we bend reality? Can we warp time?

If reality could bend and time could warp,
Would humans change their ways?
Perhaps they would, if humans could value
The potent force and splendor that is Mother Earth.

The Monsters Within

Christina Sng

You follow me everywhere

Unburdened by sealed doors
And encased windows,
Always too close
For me to escape you.

For a time I thought
You were my shadow,
But too quickly
I learned you are not.

These bloodied bodies
I wake up beside tell me
That, like me,
You are corporeal.

I hoped you would help me
Clean up your kills,
But you never appear
When you are needed.

Instead, I've become
An expert in body disposal,
For no one would believe
I did not do what you did.

Today I see you
Wearing my face
In the mirror.
I know the truth.

Mother told me the secret
In a reluctant phone call,
How we fought to the death
In her womb

While she watched,
Horrified,
Through the ultrasound.
Afterwards, I ate you.

For far too long
I have lived in your shadow.
But now, dear twin,
We are truly one.

I no longer fear you.

Doctor Fulci's Fantastic Cure for Nightmares

Liam Garriock

The esteemed Doctor Fulci had set up practice in a remote and northern mountain range that seldom receives visitors. When I say "set up practice," I mean that he converted an ancient monastery or temple into a fantastic sanitorium for those troubled by diabolical nightmares and invasive dreams, outside an empty village allegedly haunted by ghosts. Being one haunted by nightmares of a stark and profound kind, I journeyed to that desolate temple outside the haunted village in those merciless mountains, seeking salvation from the psychic terrors and grinning imps that constantly plagued me and separated me from the rest of mankind. "Doctor Fulci promises to relieve you of your inner demons through radical psychotherapy! Apply now!" Artists, poets, performers, musicians, all have seemingly benefited from Fulci's wondrous treatments, which, rumours say, combined ancient esoteric traditions, such as Tantra and Gnosticism, with gruelling and brutal physical procedures that left the body exhausted and aching.

Upon arrival at that hoary temple, that Roerich landscape kissed by high and chilling winds, emotionless orderlies, who could easily have been devilish automatons, escorted me to the Chamber of Purging, where I would be cured of my phantasies. It was a wide, round, stone-grey room, and Doctor Fulci himself, a short, pale man wearing dark glasses, stood at the side with other doctors whose expressions matched the stone interior. I was seated in a chair and made to visualise my nightmare phantasies before a large screen. My corrupted imagination, seething with horror and metaphysical lunacy, paraded before my awestruck and terrified eyes, as though my skull had been opened up to reveal the inner carnival of debauchery and cavorting chimeras. Fulci and his doctors looked on, implacable, reserved, scrutinising the images they witnessed. I remember beginning to feel weak, as though all my energy were being depleted. When it was done, and I felt quite drained, the demonic processions on the screen disappeared, and Doctor Fulci removed his glasses. Where his eyes should have been, there were merely hollow red sockets. One of the orderlies began wheeling a trolley of jars containing thick, multicoloured liquids, like rainbows of jelly, towards Fulci; he opened one, dipped his finger in the viscous, polychromatic liquid, and tasted it. "Delicious dreams," he muttered, satisfied. Almost immediately, the orderlies carted my exhausted frame and placed me in one of the guests' sleeping quarters, where I at once fell into a black and dreamless sleep.

I returned to civilisation cleansed of my nightmares, my phantasies, my howling, coalescing demons. My imagination was now a blank void, a tabula rasa, which no effulgent beings born of wonder and feeling would ever visit again. For the first time in my life, I was a wholly normal and wholly sane person, and, for the first time, I began to feel that cruel feeling we all call regret.

Temple of the Condor

(Machu Picchu)

Ann K. Schwader

No mere formation, but the outstretched wings
of something neither stone nor sky might birth,
the shadows that it casts upon this place
are not of Earth.

Men named it *condor* for its sacred scar
of darkness drawn across that upper world
where sun & moon & lightning & the stars
turn gods unfurled.

Beneath these fearsome pinions they incised
the rest in arabesques of head & beak,
suggestions of some elder entity
no tongue may speak.

Less art than abattoir, those channels cut
in replication of a raptor's might
permitted liquid sacrifice to drain
down into night.

What thirsted to receive it there remains
a source of mystery: few tourists dare
that lightless cavern guides deny, & seek
more wholesome air.

Yet when Andean mists obscure the trail
that winds to safety, wanderers & fools
still scramble through. The consequences spread
in sanguine pools.

Subterranean Hungers

David C. Kopaska-Merkel

Foundations crack, the houses lean and twist,
The summer's dry, and sinkholes open wide,
The neighbor's house and Dad's new Porsche go,
And Mr. Jones can't find his hot young bride,
The girl I dream of wetly every night.
My dad climbs down and calls and calls her name;
Then Dad stops calling out and starts to scream,
And no one else dares go into the pit.

Two paramedics, sent into the Earth,
Seek out my dad; his hoarse and weakened cries
Lead them to find him with the gnawed remains
Of Mrs. Jones, sweet goddess of my nights.
"That thing bit off her head" is all he says;
He never tells us what it was he saw.

The Great Wheel

(A Rondel)

Frank Coffman

The year's Great Wheel gives us our Sabbat days.
On Quarters and Cross-Quarters we shall meet:
On Yule the old year dies, the new we greet;
Beneath the frosts of Imbolc new life stays;
Ostara's birth of spring and greening ways
Are followed soon by Beltane's fertile heat.
The year's Great Wheel gives us our Sabbat days.
On Quarters and Cross-Quarters we shall meet:
On Litha the sun is brightest, balefires blaze;
By Lammas the god has ripened corn and wheat;
On Mabon we give thanks and drink and eat;
Dark Samhain lets us peer through Death's thick haze.
The year's Great Wheel gives us our Sabbat days.
On Quarters and Cross-Quarters we shall meet.

The Necromancer's Charm

Scott J. Couturier

A satchel of seasoned grave-soil
strung betwixt the terminating arc-bow
of clavicles makes light weight
of necromantic toil.

How oft have I been out rooting
in the cairn-yard, with wildly flinging
blaspheming spade?
Yet no spirit nor mortal molests my looting.

A pinch of blood-hallowed dirt
eases the act of exhumation,
sanctifies the rending
of wan funereal shroud—unopposed,
I lug my putrid winnings to an isolate yurt.

There, on an altar ill-starred,
graven of flame-stained femora
I incant uncouth animacy to tissues worm-rent.
Posthumous fluids run to a virulent mard.

& yet, out amongst the stark tumuli
where I scavenge nightly
I stride unimpeded, though my perverse works
are widely known & feared—
for my stalking shade they cannot descry.

The night is mine to gnaw like an archaic bone.
Prostrate, I quaff the sacral drought of coffin-drippings.
About my neck hangs the soil packet, heavy,
imbued with virginal life-pulse—
thus with exsanguinate blessings I roam
as stealthy as air & as silent as stone.

Tomb without Walls

Ross Balcom

swallowed
by the tomb

a tomb
without walls

death's
vast empire

a galaxy
of corpses

dark bodies
whirling

black tongues
singing hymns

to rot
and corruption

to the worm,
to the beetle

green light
of putrescence

the shimmering
skull

poison light,
darkness

infinite
the tomb

the necro-verse,
the universe

the tomb, the tomb,
the tomb. . . .

The Final Scrawl

Pat Calhoun

The wall claws my back as I await the
Word that will end the world. Pancho Villa
Smiles, but dark things are dancing in his eyes;
I close mine and Carcosa's towers rise—
But they are lies that the bullets will end.
He shouts; rifles roar; time seems to suspend;
After seconds like eons I look and see
Villa and the soldiers laughing at me:
"We don't shoot poets down here, Señor Bierce;
They aimed high." Now the dawn turns glorious;
Cacti raise emerald arms to the sky
In praise of life; exultant air bathes my
Body and soul. I shut my eyes to dream
For a moment, but then hear Villa's scream
Bring thunder and pain, and I can but fall.
Blood on adobe is my final scrawl.

The Jack-o'-Lantern Hearted

K. A. Opperman

The jack-o'-lantern hearted,
Whom autumn calls her own,
The all too soon departed,
The lost and the alone,
We know the way to Fairy,
Beyond October's gate,
And we will not long tarry
While twilight grows so late.

The jack-o'-lantern hearted,
The autumn's cursèd kin,
The paramour's long parted,
The wan, the worn, and thin,
We know the way to Fairy,
Just down the country lane—
We'll soon be making merry,
And come here not again.

The Vampire-Need

Cecelia Hopkins-Drewer

Blood
Is their
Burning need.
A thrill to take,
Dreadful thirst to quench.
But do they give,
Any thought
For their
Prey?

The Duke of Balladry

Adam Bolivar

On Balladry, the Sapphire Isle,
    A castle, ruined, stands,
A haunted brooding ancient pile,
    Upon bejewelled sands.

He is the Duke of Balladry,
    The master of this isle,
Whose name resounds in legendry,
    And regal is his style,

For secretly, as ravens know,
    He is the King of Nod,
His ballads known to any crow,
    And widely are they cawed.

While underneath and in the end,
    His secret name is Jack:
To dreamers all he is a friend,
    Who tread the Ancient Track.

Disclosure

Norbert Góra

A horror can be seen
above the city,
vibrating tentacles
illuminated by the snow,
winter wind
accompanied by the screams;
is the conflagration coming,
is the end of human dreams?

A nightmare that has no name
hangs over us like an ax.
What is the purpose of the prayers?
It is not as sacred as a pax,
revelation of the end of our days,
closer and closer to the ground,
the prophets heralded it differently,
but death has been finally found.

Guillotined

A Horror Story in Haiku

Carl E. Reed

Snicketing whisper-lick:
cold steel sheering shocked flesh
muscle, marrow, bone.

Crowd & sky revolve
spattering blood, frenzied thoughts
falling severed head.

Sodden thump into
ensanguined wicker basket—
wide eyes, open mouth.

Altar of Yig

David Barker

Of the Abbey's lay brothers, I was the lowest, admitted by grace when I begged at the door. The abbot allowed me to tend the library, shelving codices used by monastics. Those vellum-bound tomes he forbade me to read. The script in one of them I could decipher when found on a table, its pages laid open. Fearful of raising the wrath of our Abbot, I snapped shut the codex and locked its gold clasp. Yet ere it was closed, a brief script I saw, and uttered it under my breath as I worked. Thus passed my days in mild contemplation, when suddenly, one noon, a crisis arose. Our order was struck by a fierce horde of heathens. They slaughtered my brethren and pillaged the archive, toppling cases and torching the books. In terror I fled to the chapel—abandoned—past the sanctuary to the Altar of Yig. From a wall thrice my height, a domed ridge extended. A wandering friar named it Spine of the Serpent. A marvel illicit, it now lay untended, no monks being present to halt my approach. If I were caught, my transgression meant death. Extending a hand, I touched its deep polish, while echoed nearby my brothers' death throes. I'd heard whispered rumors of monks at the altar, backbone pressing adamantine. If they were worthy, power flowed up the column. It surged through their bodies, a bright lightning bolt. Thus were they granted sublime ecstasy. Such license I seized, posed erect at the column. My spine at the Serpent's, its vigor flowed past me. But woe unto me, presumptuous sinner, found wanting, my wicked form bent to one side. In shame I broke off and fled from Yig's Altar. Through smoldering ashes I ran from the abbey, while clutched in my cloak was treasure divine. From library ruins I saved but one volume: the gold-clasped codex, untouched by flame. That wisdom I stole from the scene of destruction, lore to render me favored by Yig.

Poe

Randall D. Larson

Mortared tombs of stone,
The raven, the ape, the cat:
Tangible terrors.

A lost love, mourning,
The grotesque and arabesque;
Unending despair.

A great House shall fall,
A grue-haunted labyrinth,
Nightmares unending.

Haruspex

4 haiku

Geoffrey A. Landis

Raindrops patter
secret messages in Morse code
telling the future.

Three black birds fly north
against a spotless blue sky:
I weep for us all.

I read my future
in patterns of cracked concrete
and the wind's soft voice.

I read my future
in entrails and blood stains—
a short one: my own.

The Secret Pool

Darrell Schweitzer

I know a place deep in the woods
where a black, crumbling crater sinks down
to a still, shining pool,
and there's a girl in it, long past dead,
her hair a clotted mass,
her face dissolving like some discarded vegetable.
I'm there too, not a reflection, but in the pool with her,
the two of us embracing like lovers
who have forgotten all joy, anger, lust, and passion,
the memory of our lives no more than the twinge
an amputee might feel from a phantom limb.
I stare for hours, until with the utmost effort
I am finally able to ascend from that particular Avernus,
clawing at the dank earth, craving the light.
Then I try to convince myself it was all a dream, nothing more,
until the compulsion overcomes me once again,
and I must descend for another look.

As One Poet to Another

G. Sutton Breiding

To D. Sidney-Fryer, 21 March 2019.

a clock is ticking somewhere in my head
in a dream in a Martian thrift shop
it is very early and very late
I smell cinnamon and sex
notebooks papers books all over
strange notes from across the river
my pen awaits   is that death's harp
a thing remains but what   my mother's voice
the languages I might still uncover
in a found poem   a sonnet of dust and keratosis
biopsies and rotten lungs
diesel fumes and gravel   like some strange muses
the hair of an ancient undine
coffee and Morgantown   listening to my heart
working always a bit overtime
old runes for new magic   turtle mind
"when the air was gold with honeybees
and time was an endless childhood"
I wrote a thousand years ago—
light years and salamanders
hollows covered in trilliums
fallen from the moon and kissed by half-wild girls

insane world of humans

I have written some things
ill desperado of the marshes
phantom of parks and pre-dawn streets
what's left of a non-winter sliding like cinders
into another surreal spring
the redbud lips of quicksilver muses
to write a letter!
to never see a fox again
bluebells send out their ghastly telegrams
floaters and auras of another realm of (un)being
philosophy of the lichen
"what the fuck am I doing here?"
the eternal question or not so eternal
the sorcerer masturbates
a spell or two   a hissing in the ears
is that a lamia or a nerve disorder
on streets of doddering seniors
a porcelain sadness   where is my vocabulary

the moon of unicorns
still rising over these black and tortured hills
the music of dead lilies
in the 3 a.m. living room

I have shat in outhouses and holes in the woods

and a thousand toilets of time and space
in my astronaut's suit
on days of autumn glory
(writing letters quietly
in a twentieth-century light)
O the misty distances the hazy shades
the terrible strangeness of this place
Old Age   an ill-fitting suit of skin
on burning bones   going blind and crazy
where is my iron lung   raven seers
dryads all over me
as I cough my way to an orgasm
paranormal ghost   explosions
ectoplasmic semen   floating
the golden seed of the Poet
left behind in the meadows
I am great as the cicada is great
that is enough

She Tasted of Gin and Death

Curtis M. Lawson

Our lips met in a swirl of toxic mist,
In a black sea of coldest dispassion;
She tasted of gin and death when we kissed.

A lost, lonely soul, she wouldn't be missed;
She was known to sell carnal distraction.
Our lips met in a swirl of toxic mist.

We walked the beach where old spirits exist.
In the fog we made love, in a fashion;
She tasted of gin and death when we kissed.

Dead-souled and drunk, still she clawed and she hissed,
But the sea filled her and she turned ashen.
Our lips met in a swirl of toxic mist.

Even when she stilled I could not resist.
I placed my lips upon her cold passion;
She tasted of gin and death when we kissed.

Years passed and that ghast formed from gas that hissed;
Her eyes were blackest seas of dispassion.
She tasted of gin and death when kissed;
Our lips met in a swirl of toxic mist.

Vampire Vigil

Manuel Arenas

Slumped in a Luther chair, Adalbert Glöde, failing in his vigil, dozes and dreams of his inamorata, the Vampiress Morbidezza Vespertilio, who lies, quiescent, in her ebon coffin on an inky, satin-draped catafalque. Initially resolved to descry the stir of vitality in her marmoreal mien, he has instead nodded off, dreaming of her sepulchral pulchritude and wicked wiles. He longs to kiss her luring red lips and rekindle the vivifying ardor in her gelid breast, melting the preternatural derma-frost, returning her milk-white flesh to its connatural suppleness that is consistent with her appellation, but dares not for fear of contamination from her unhallowed contagion. He craves her acknowledgment of the asseveration of his love, but her ire at his treachery will not allow for it. Believing her stuck in the pall between worlds of the living and the dead, he dreams that he seeks her accurst shade in the Underworld but has gone astray, meandering in the Mournful Fields. He calls her name, but the only response amidst the keening din of the disconsolate shades of unrequited and slain lovers is the tinkling of his ladylove's spinet and the doleful ayre of a turtledove.

Wandering aimlessly through the bleak shadowland, he spies the shade of his other victim, the Graf von Totenlaut, whom he smote when he spirited away his consort, that undead Delilah, lumbering amidst the pitiless fallow glebe-land bearing his severed head. He halts a-sudden and holds his head aloft from its raven locks, like a lantern, scanning the woebegone terrain till his bitter, silvery orbs rest upon Adalbert like fulgurating stars gazing down with fierce discernment. As the rent in his albescent breast gushes precipitously his heart's blood in a torrent, his gaunt, livid visage opens its fang-barbed lips to cry his slayer's name, "Adalbert!"

But the voice emitted from his ghastly maw is not the grave baritone of the once stately count, but rather the mellifluous, albeit minacious, intonations of his bewitching relict, the exquisite fallen angel whose name is synonymous with death-warmed delicacy, yet whose heart is as black and implacable as the dreams of Death. He hears the voice again, but this time from all around him, as the articulation of a lowering deity lording over him from above. Straining his eyes in the adumbration, he tries to locate the source of the utterance. As oft happens in the absurd realm of dreams, the unlikely spectacle of the sanguinary cataract swelled into a deluge, flooding the fallow ground and overwhelming the spurned cavalier, covering him up to his neck briefly as he heard his name called once more before succumbing to the gory wave.

Waking with a start, Adalbert struggles to focus his bleary blue eyes to the grisly candlelit spectacle on his lap: a twined crimson mantle atop which is perched a mangled and masticated bird's head, a turtledove.

"Morbidezza!" he cries.

"*Sono qui,*" returned the voice of Doom.

The Thing That Watches While I Write

Thomas Tyrrell

Beyond my desk-lamp's arc of light,
the thing that watches while I write
lurks in the darkness of the room.
Its bleak eyes glitter in the gloom
like starlight on a stagnant lake;
and whether I should sleep or wake
those eyes are all I see of it,
cold, incorporeal eyes that flit
between the shadows swift as imps.
I never seem to catch a glimpse
of scales or fur or flesh, to place
those formless orbs within a face
and give the thing a settled shape.
The fine hairs prickle on my nape,
my fingers clench around the pen,
my prose stalls in mid-sentence, when
I feel those awful eyes on me.

And then, involuntarily,
imagination starts to form
a crowd of images—a swarm
of monstrous visions from the air
around that sharp, unblinking stare.
Wild spectres dance before my sight:

the maenad, rapt with wild delight
to eat raw meat and drink hot blood,
who tossed into the Hebrus flood
the head of Orpheus, and tore
his flesh to shreds with tooth and claw;
the gloating troll beneath the arch
who listens as the soldiers march
to war across his parapet;
more indistinct and monstrous yet
the nameless nightmares out of space
who look upon the human race
as so much vermin to be culled.
My weary wits are spent and dulled,
as blocked and stalled and incomplete
I leave my nightly torture-seat,
drained, empty, void of word and will.
The thing remains and watches still.

Plague's Wake

Ashley Dioses

The barren land was still,
And not a sound was made.
The plague brought death with skill,
And it refused to fade.

No single wolf did howl;
No raven called its caw;
No cat's desirous yowl;
No humans at the saw.

At first it took a town
And conquered next a city.
The plague would not back down
And felt no trace of pity.

What followed in its wake,
Those left would not forget—
The lives the plague did take,
And its persistent threat.

It left a single mark
At first, with just one touch.
So soon the eyes turned dark,
Then they were in Death's clutch.

It swallowed up hoarse screams,
Then all were without life.
Now light no longer gleams
In eyes touched by Death's knife.

The mark was just the start;
A kiss then, on pale lips.
It traveled to the heart
And left it a cold crypt.

To a Cat-Daemon: A Litany of Antient Ægypt

Manuel Pérez-Campos

Thou who art as profligate & as abolish'd
as an irrational number—what impalpable
power has sent thee? Why art thou always waiting
ahead sitting overbold with crepuscular
gloom high upon funereal statuary
as I walk down the ramp to the burial chamber
where I am to embalm the latest labourer
lover of Nitokris? And when night's shadowing
of the misshapen Androsphinx turns tall
as it blocks bright dunes tumbling out of the daystar,
why dost thou appear like a phantom of ebony
on my bar'd chest as I lie in my hovel, anguish'd
by yesterday's laggard calour? Nightmare creature
of the lotophagi—why am I mir'd with thee
e'en as I lave by the plenilune Nile's nenuphar?
What termagant, doom'd to begging through the coveting
of Nitokris, has chaunted my death to me
for lifting her lowly husband to athanasy?

Methuselah

Wade German

Relentless, like the wrath of God,
The great epochal cycles turn.
I've watched their motion, rapt and awed,
Seeing all things in time return
To render meaningless all change . . .
All things to me seem still and strange.

Down the dark eons, age on age,
I've witnessed wickedness and wept,
Seeing my kindred on each wage
Recurrent nightmares, as if they slept:
False hearts, false faiths, false tongues, false deeds—
From them, abomination breeds . . .

Weary of evil, weak and grey,
I watch my children build my tomb;
At last I smell my own decay . . .
But I shall greet my welcome doom,
Leaving the truth of all I've seen:
The human race should not have been—

Lord, how I've come to hate them all,
The symptom of the universe!
Heaven, I pray you hear my call
And heed my prayer, a parting curse:
That God on them a deluge sends,
That human filth from Earth is cleansed.

Cassandra Can't Tell You

Allan Rozinski

Cryptic Cassandra, augury's cursed bride,
warned of the shape of things to come
in a manner that never seemed to sidestep
the inevitable. Is it that, even were we shown a map
to spy where future perils and pitfalls lie,
absent the experience of the journey itself
we would all still be as blind as if
Cassandra herself
had told us of our fate?

And take all the oracles of Delphi and ask
each after they cleanse themselves
in the cold Castalian waters,
and breathe in the sweet vapors
rising from the temple's floor
that open the gates of perception
to receive the gift of divination,
where it is hoped that all the answers
to the mysteries of chance and circumstance
are waiting to be found: then the
questions come, one by one,
each an echo of the other,
from the endless procession of supplicants
seeking to escape their fate.

*   *   *

Chaos further feeds and grows
when attempts are made to impose
blind order on its resistive and ungovernable
tendencies.

Heraclitus said, "You cannot step
into the same river twice."

Trojan Horses
await us all.

Lair of the Bat People

Ross Balcom

smell of guano,
beating of wings

voices
calling your name

lair of the bat people

caves and passages
older than time

fool, you followed
the emerald light

the inner world
the inner sky

the emerald moon
cold its rays

lair of the bat people

the empty throne
for you it waits

your subjects
greet you

"We hail you,
    O Wingless One!"

this your destiny
there is no other

lord of the bat people

your kingdom
claims you

now and forever
lord

of the winged horde!

Reparation

Christina Sng

Yesterday you walked
In your skin and your bones
As you breathed out poison,
Destroying families and homes.

You care nothing
For the roadkill in your wake,
But for the skins you'd take
And the fur that you'd make.

See my scythe,
Keep it in your eye.
Now see your body
Lying in the sty.

We have moved
To the sacred place in the sky,
Watching you weep,
Watching you die.

In the Days of the Vertical Ocean

David C. Kopaska-Merkel

When seas streamed off the edge of pancake earth,
And water boiled against God's rocky jaws,
Where mermaids, teeth phalanxes white as snow,
Adorned their hair with sailors' ivory,
And sirens sang us past the turning point,
Well, it was long past time to set all sails,
To jettison the stuff we didn't need,
And squint into the hellish void-born wind.

I struck a pose behind the useless wheel,
While stars of which no living man has told
In horizontal lands shone bright below,
And dragons gone for centuries from lands
We knew plucked screaming men right off our deck,
I thought of you, and wished you here with me.

The Underwater Circus

Kurt Newton

"Come down by the lakeside,"
  called the circus clown with his sad-faced makeup on.

The curious were drawn as nighttime fell,
  like moths to the colored lights, the carousel.

My brother tagged along, and I was drawn as well.
  We saw the lights, we heard the music, and something else.

A sound found only on the radio,
  in between stations where the static pools and the emptiness dwells.

And still we followed like all the rest,
  past the sad-faced clown to the water's edge.

And there beneath the surface
  swam the multicolored shimmer of the underwater circus.

There was no price of admission,
  just the light of our souls to keep the rides spinning.

I watched in horror as each by each,
  the town's people sank to the bottom to the circus beneath.

But when I felt the cold water
  creep over my skin, I turned to my brother.

"Grab some mud and plug your ears
and run, there's something evil happening here!"

Now evil is a strong word and I was still young;
what's evil to others can be beautiful to some.

I'd like to say I saved both my brother
and me that day, but only one of us escaped the water.

And it was as beautiful as advertised,
the sounds in my ears, the lights in my eyes.

There were circus animals with cotton-candy wings,
swimming circles above the crowds and everything.

There was music all around as if in a dream,
and laughter so loud it could be mistaken for screams.

I knew my brother and I were not the same;
I was more spirited while he played it safe.

So I sank to the bottom to join the rest,
on the long carousel ride of death.

And I've been here, now, for fifty years this way,
each year a different town, a different lake.

So if you see a clown one day
calling, "Come down by the lakeside"—run away!

But if you have no fear of what lies beneath the surface,
come join us here at the underwater circus.

Super-Position

Ron L. Johnson II

Take a drink from the cup of mind,
Pour it out all over space-time,
Transport your body elsewhere,
but still, somehow, be here and there.

Be like the sub-atomic particle
that can quantum-super-position,
and do it with precision.

The Absence of Clouds

G. O. Clark

The cemetery is dead,
its grass brown and brittle,
the unceasing drought
sparing neither the dead
nor the living.

In the groundskeeper's
shed a riding mower rusts,
blades still crusted with grass
once green, skeleton slumped
over its steering wheel.

Some headstones have
unwillingly toppled over,
but most still stand upright,
defying gravity like the dead
beneath before dying.

Their epitaphs linger,
weathered over time, their
messages varied as those they
memorialize; decades passing,
eyes gone to dust.

The cemetery stretches
for miles beyond its rusted
iron gates; the city a mausoleum,
crucible-sun shining down through
an absence of clouds.

Divided by Demons

Mary Krawczak Wilson

You had one foot in the bright
Halcyon days of boyhood
And one foot in the dense wood
Where the Elders alighted in the night.

You came from an iridescent island
Where rare flowers suffused the air
And lulled you far away from there
To an inchoate and arid land.

You yearned to aspire and ascend
To an intense and illuminating place.
Instead, you descended into a nether space
Alone, insentient, and unable to comprehend.

You were found on a desolate beach
Where vultures heeded the carrion call
By plucking out your blind eyeball
Until it rolled into the sea—forever out of reach.

Down the Garden Path

M. F. Webb

The garden with its iron gate ajar
Invites you, and you readily accept
A walk upon its path, its grass a-star
With daisies, hemmed with roses richly kept.

Before you, shadows lush and humid fall
And rhododendrons complicate the light.
Crooked toadstools sprout beneath their pall
And foxgloves loom from unexpected height.

Lilies and narcissus gasp perfume
Their pallid blooms like strange corroded gems.
You turn at sudden step within the gloom—
A gloved hand seizes fast a bleeding stem.

No friend is it who in the ivy waits.
You glance ahead. There is no exit gate.

The God of Phlegm

Maxwell Gold

I heard hollow empty tones echo in the night as the dark hymns of corroded wheels danced across silver rails. Their oxidized feet tapped along with magnetic electrification over the bars, as orange flakes of rust drifted off toward the purple horizon. Snaking along miles of once bustling track, these now hulking monsters carried nothing but empty promises and dead ideals, in the form of a submissive populace with no way out from behind the dripping iron teeth that lined its black wooden frame. The railways were the veins of an empire, a bloodline that filled a silver world with the hopes and dreams of glittering progress, where their ancestors rode with a pristine and gallant speed, like the greatest of stallions. A dominant evil force took hold, corrupting the world. Its grip, filled with a cyberlust vexing even the best of men, devastated their minds with ravaging erotic untruths, while leaving them satisfied in the interim with a ghastly misinformed reality. The trains became an unholy salvation, a gateway to a place beyond their defiled bed, toward a station of reactionary pragmatism.

The windows of the station rattled with each voiceless scream, every whistle and pleasurable howl as the moment approached. I knew the monstrous thing was near, and soon it would be my turn to step on board, despite my terrifying reluctance. Past the ruined obsidian palaces and marbled side streets where neon dreams were wrapped inside Teflon robes, stuffed in steel boxes sold to the highest bidder by way of some dark fulfillment. On the backs of a serpentine ironclad leviathan, I could feel a sense of doom wrap its long bony fingers around the station as the fog rolled in and the whistle howled once more. There was no conductor, no driver or being controlling this thing, only a force of will as its rusted wheels screeched to a halt.

Underneath the billowing clouds of ash, fire, and fallen dreams, I helplessly wandered toward the platform as the train released a breath of delightful toxicity. While the moans and pleas from those clamoring behind its crooked teeth were awful and chilling, I could not resist my carnal urges as the wooden doors slid open and the mechanized beast lazily sat on its metal bed. This new god, Nath'Zrath the Demented God of Phlegm, an offspring of those devilish Cyber Things, had crept throughout the world leaving a trail of schizophrenic idealisms in its wake. As its teeth clamped shut around me, I knew there was nothing to be certain of anymore.

Cruel Eleanora

Adam Bolivar

Once Eleanora schemed to wed
    Her sister's suitor Jack,
And sent her to a river bed
    To end her life, alack.

But on the wedding day there came
    A wayward balladeer,
Whose ballads garnered spreading fame
    That rumoured him a seer.

He had a harp of bones he made
    From Elspeth's grim remains,
Which in the river had decayed,
    For time our flesh disdains.

This harp was haunted and decried
    Her murder, drowned and cold;
Then all there knew how Elspeth died:
    A dismal story told.

Cruel Eleanora fled from there,
    In shame and in disgrace,
A streak ran through her raven hair,
    And malice marked her face.

A sorceress she now became,
    And dwelt in tangled thorn;
Her wickedness brought her dark fame,
    Yet still she was forlorn.

She learned about the Ballad Stone,
    A sapphire steeped in doom,
And vowed to make it hers alone,
    A jewel to suit her gloom.

She sent an owl, its talons sharp,
    To soar across Lake Nod,
To where the Duke a-played his harp
    With no one to applaud.

And when the Duke fell fast asleep
    On ballads drunk, and wine;
The stone was stolen from his keep,
    A master-stroke malign.

The Duke of Ballads then awoke
    To find his treasure gone,
And tears his silk cravat would soak
    As broke the hated dawn.

Tears of the Raven

Christopher Collingwood

A black feather lies on a virgin grave
Fresh tear drops ache to wilted petals
A youthful yearning hangs in the wind
Old men pass but do not stop to remember
Death is too fresh a companion
Echoes of lost dreams call out to the wind
A raven lands on the restless grave
Its beady eyes reflect the shadow of a man
A memory of a child, cries to the tombstone
A lost love shivers beneath the cold moon
Unattained dreams drop like ashes of agony
Regret reaches out to its silent watcher
False hope stands in a cloak of despair
The raven seeks no audience with the tormented
It cannot shed a tear for each lost soul
Or the world would drown in a sea of mourning
A black cat is unsettled in its wanderings
For the soul seeks to barter with a familiar traveler
But madness forever tumbles in a shallow grave
Cherished memories spill like grains into nothingness
The raven caws to the lost wanderer
It scratches at the grave to commune with the dead
A man stands under the shadow of the raven
Feathers envelop him into the final moment
He begins walking through a playground

A vacant swing signals the end of his innocence
He enters his car
The playground is covered by an unkindness of ravens
The wheels screech as the car crashes
A raven stares at him through the broken windscreen
Memories burn like weltered ambers
He stares deeply into the eyes of a raven
And sees his life through the eyes of the silent watcher
He experiences a profound awakening in the echoing of the caw
Feathers emerge from within his memories
Until he realises that he has become the raven
The raven stops scratching at the grave
Silence is welcomed by the moonlight
The raven knows the moment has passed
It takes flight into the night.

Graveyard of the Gods

Scott J. Couturier

I heard rumor the Old Gods were dead:
those oft told of in druid-hymn & story.
I heard it wrothly muttered in El Ad Mied,
in taverns clinging to her quayed promontory
like barnacles cleave to a leviathan's hide:
Like a leviathan is that city, abyssal jaws wide.

From that *polis* of a thousand, thousand ships
I set forth in a shabby, weather-wracked barque,
desirous to assess the Gods' ambrosial lips
& eyes: surely there yet lingered some vital spark!
I sailed from the Bay of Twilit Delights
forth onto the Ocean of Unending Nights.

There, through storm-winds of supernal force,
I passed beyond where most men willingly sail:
hand to the tiller, maintaining my course
past black islets whose sirens forsakenly wail.
Beyond the gloaming of high onyx tombs
the gray Walls of the World indefatigably loom.

Eyes fixed devoutly on the Southern Star
I paid no heed to the snapping, uncouth things
that the glass-clear waters riotously marred
with lashing tails & element-aberrant wings.

Against waves waged I a merry, half-mad war—
far in the east espied I the Old Gods' shore.

At last I could perceive their pitiable wreck.
Like sundered idols hewn of luminous gem
each God was severed cleanly at hand & neck:
about them grew blood poppies, fat on stem.
Lowering the tempest-tried sails of my barque
I hove closer to shore, seeking for their spark.

Cavern-hollow were all their eyes & throats.
Their limbs were twisted, greening with moss.
In the recess of each sovereign skull wove motes
of mortal souls mourning for Immortal loss.
Great God-corpses, haphazardly heaped on the shore:
timeless monuments to Time's pitiless spore.

Landing, I wandered amongst cages of bones.
Profane scavengers dwelt there: I heeded them not.
The wind raised a dirge of unthroated moans
as the sun waned to Night's omnipotent blot.
In the darkness, ghouls crept forth & ravenously fed
on the marrow of Gods, now divinely dead.

At length plucked I loose an unlighted stone
from out one of those breathless titan's breasts.

Held up to starlight, it glimmered & shone
with a fabulous fire half-recalled, thrice-blessed.
Thus with the incandescent dead heart of a God
I boarded my barque & set sail, soul rue & roughshod.

Returned I at last to the mortal-haunted world.
The scarred, cynical sailors of El Ad Mied
welcomed affirmation of the Old Gods' netherworld—
they had told me, *after all*, that they were dead.
Went I to a tavern, where I downed many an ale—
in rotgut stupor dreamed I of a gleaming white sail.

A pilgrim went willing to the Walls of the World,
sailing a savage wind nameless on material charts.
His eye steely, fingers convulsively curled
around a dead god's cold, insentient heart:
he went to hew a grave-marker to the Gods of Old.
His own skin was of marble, his own heart flint-cold.

Reaching at last those colossus-strewn shores,
he erected a cinnabar stone, red as a clot.
Cut he letters with a blade of extraterrestrial ore—
& thus was graven on the marker of that burial plot:
"What once was Celestial is now rendered Clay.
  Mankind slays all Gods: It was ever Their way."

Solving for X

Ann K. Schwader

So now our wise astronomers deny
a need for Planet X. Whatever force
is pulling distant planetoids off-course
need not be singular & shadowed. Why,
an orbiting of icy pebbles might
suffice as well. Less drama & less fuss
means sounder science, separating us
from morbid fascination with some night
beyond our logic. Only dreams insist
upon a whisper of crustacean wings
above the Yuggoth hives—& what they bring
in certain strange containers that resist
all waking understanding, as they keep
the weight of nightmare tugging at our sleep.

The Demon Ball

Tatiana Strange

Deep in the forest in the dark of night
There is a secret place cloaked in dread,
Hidden far from human eyes,
Where the living fear to tread.

Every once in a while on a full moon they gather
In a dark castle tucked away snug in the woods,
For the Demon Ball they meet together to rejoice their love of darkness and
    gloom.

From all corners of the Earth they come;
The undead ride in carriages of black,
Drawn by nightmares, dead horses with glassy eyes,
Galloping down the dark roads mindlessly as the flesh wears away from their
    legs and backs.

As the guests stream into the castle they are greeted by skeletons at the doors;
Witches dance around a pyre and music fills the darkened halls;
Above the tables priests are hung, bound and gagged,
Whose throats have been slit and bled to fill the glasses.

The shadows of ghosts lurk about
As ghouls and spiders clamber along the walls,
And screeching demons swirl around the ceiling above
At the hellish Demon Ball.

Night-creatures howl from the forest outside while strange moans echo from the
    halls;
The shadows of the witches dance around the fire as the darkness embraces
    them all.

The skeletons serve them glasses of blood,
Their bony smiles permanent leers;
The ghouls snarl and cackle at the spectacle,
The guests jest in macabre cheer.

Together they are bound in darkness, all these creatures of the night.
Slowly one after the other they depart in silence before the first morning light;
The fading moon glows solemnly over the castle walls . . .

The guests return once more to their dark and lonesome abodes,
Knowing that in time they will once again gather and dance and feast at the
    Demon Ball.

The Bog Man

Chelsea Arrington

The fens are dark and dank and deep.
An eldritch fire will flit and float,
Enticing men to deathly sleep
In graves of mud and lands remote.

An evil shudder ripples out
From deep inside the boggy-bog.
The villagers all have no doubt
That doom will come with next day's fog.

They sacrifice a sow and cock
And plead to gods of fire and sea.
They cry and spit; on wood they knock
To free themselves of what will be.

But deep within the bubbling ooze
A monster wakes from ancient sleep.
The villagers he must abuse;
His curse he must fulfill and keep.

A man he was of twenty-one
When forced to greet an early doom.
A sacrifice, his life was done;
An offering to dark and gloom.

His voice rang out before he died:
A curse to haunt the land when he

Should one day rise to take his bride
From those who would not set him free:

"My curse I lay upon you all!
One day I shall return for blood!
A daughter shall become my thrall;
A bride for me in deepest mud!"

The villagers have lived in fear
Awaiting this unholy day.
They sense their time is drawing near.
He stirs from depths of black and grey.

A monster he, both foul and grim;
He walks toward the village square.
It's gloaming time, the light is dim.
A maid he spies with golden hair.

With not a word he picks her up
And drags her to the marriage bed.
The villagers were all at sup;
They could not see the tears she shed.

And so they sleep, a groom and wife
Within the deepest boggy-bog.
An otherworldly, dreamless life;
Their shroud: the mud, the trees, and fog.

On Gustave Moreau's Canvas
The Apparition

Manuel Pérez-Campos

Dripping drops of pale, desert-tempered blood,
the Baptist's head soars achingly to laughter
from filigree-brocaded sycophants
at Salomé's behest: compelled by magical
art, it moans a blasphemy in mid-air
and winks at her: and lo, in that chamber
exalted through black notes of bawdy license
where peacocks' feathers and argent tiaras
rule, and from which is barred the Baptist's god,
his voice rues—yet as hers, no longer deep.
Garbed in lithe gossamer of twilit azure
that delights the senses, she who showcases
her daemonic powers dawdles until
laughter subsides not, and seraphim weep.

Black-Tongue Kiss

Carl E. Reed

Part I

They buried me in a shallow grave;
    I moaned & writhed & cried
out for a mercy the murdering spade
    cold blued steel—denied.

My favorite glass on the dinner table:
    arsenic in the wine.
I drank it unknowing; Art licking his lips,
    my wife's voice low & kind.

"I'm sorry, darling; I truly am,"
    Beth sighed with glistening eye;
"but it just isn't working; I'm terribly bored.
    So my love—my dear—goodbye."

I struggled to speak, but vile poison
    had toppled me out of the chair;
rictused fingers clawed at my throat;
    friend Art, a hand in my hair,

dragged me kicking & choking across the floor,
    out the door to the yard & the spade—
& there, beneath a bone-white moon,
    Beth cudgeled me dead in the grave.

Beth cudgeled me dead in the grave, her eyes
    lambent & soft as red firefly light
that *zigzig* flickers an instant & dies—
     Beth cudgeled me dead in the grave.

Part II

The voice of the void is an idiot hiss—
    no color, blacker than black;
how long I lay dead I can only conjecture;
    I awoke in the Earth to the crack

of thunder that followed the rivening bolt:
    lightning struck the oak
beneath which I lie buried; I clawed at the dirt,
    cold, fungus'd, moldered—rain-soaked.

O! the thing that arose to the cry of the loons
    there on the shore of the lake
by the white picket fence of the bay-windowed home
    was a tottering wreck that would make

the stoutest heart quaver; a strong mind break.
    I shivered & groaned in despair;
skeletal claws sieved flesh to the sod—
    I scratched at what wasn't much there.

I took a step forward—fell—rose again.
    To the house! A foot . . . one foot more;
& thus by degrees I lurched 'cross the space
    'twixt the grave & my Christmas-wreathed door.

My teeth were clenched in rictus grim;
    I fancied infernal seraphim
looked on with foul & impish grins
    as my knuckles rap-rapped on the door.

Part III

Thrice did I knock, while inside I heard
    a low mutter of words & approaching tread;
the door flung open—"Art," I said,
    "what comfort have you for the dead?"

My cuckolding friend reeled backward in shock;
    he cursed & ran for the gun
Beth kept in the dresser beside the bed
    in which we'd conceived a son.

I followed Art into the master bedroom;
    my wife sat up reading in bed,
paperback falling from nerveless fingers.
    "Michael. *My god!* You're dead."

Beth's eyes were wild & fever-bright;
     I spoke from worm-clotted throat:
"Lightning brought back what steel put down:
     now endeth all light & hope.

"How could you do it? How long did you scheme?
     How many times over the plan
did you pore with my friend to ensure you're enriched—
     you bitch!—by two hundred grand?"

Art found the revolver; wheeled & fired—
     the flash from the barrel cold heat
imparted to bullets that ripped through my chest,
     walls, door, & Christmas wreath.

Again & again Art fired until
     the gun *click-clicked* in his hand;
"It's empty, you fool!" I snarled, advanced—
     slapped his face, said, "Hear my demand—

"Life-for-life: the only law
     that wipes a murderous gloat
straight off the face of men who kill
     other men." I tore out his throat.

Art gurgled & staggered; a fount of blood
    hit the hideous rot of my face;
Beth threw off the covers, jumped to her feet,
    intent on fleeing that space.

"Hold, my darling." & that's just what I did—
    I took my wife in my arms
& left her dead on the floor—last kiss:
    black-tongued, green-moldered, red-wormed.

I took my shrieking wife in my arms;
    Beth clawed & kicked, but no further harm
could be done to one who'd succumbed to her charms—
    I left her cold dead on the floor.

Diner of Delights

Claire Smith

They're alone in unknown woods, scolded:
Thrown out of their comfortable home,
Thrown out of their father's favour,
Thrown out of their stepmother's Chevrolet.

I boil up false fudge bricks;
A door to open up with liquorice slats;
And windows framed by sticks of rock;
I add a roof of gingerbread tiles.

Make our rustic hut into a diner of delights—
I cook doughnuts with custard centres;
Waffles with cream and raspberry sauce,
Bake up cupcakes piped with white icing

In paper-striped cases. My wife changes
Clothes—innocence with its green swing dress;
Yellow daisies grow over its cotton skirt;
A frilled apron tops off her costume.

Her cheeks are rouged, eyelashes curled,
Lips planted with a pouting smile—
Seeds sown to make her a doting aunt.
They tap at the door hesitant, afraid, lost . . .

We have sweets to delight, enthuse,
Satisfy both the young fools' appetites.
The boy with his Gibson guitar;
The girl and her pastel-pink hair ribbons,

Bows on her socks slipped under Mary-Janes.
We keep them both, canaries in a cage—
They chirrup along while Chuck Berry plays,
Buddy Holly, and Elvis on our jukebox.

They miss their chances to escape.
On purpose we spoil them: give Hershey bars,
All sorts of penny candies, licorice strips.
Our birds now part of the furniture;

Our dainty canaries—chirrup a song.
Who would suspect they helped us make
the forest ring? A Chevrolet cry from dents
Dished out, with sticks, over its body?

Who prepared their evil stepmother
To be served succulent as beef burgers?
With fries, and rolls; plus salsa—
to add an extra kick!

Inquiry Regarding the Dead

David Barker

1.

Your late lover,
does she hover
near the cover?

Does she crawl
down the hall
in a thrall?

A dark cloud,
is she proud
in her shroud?

Does her lust
raise the dust
and the must?

2.

Do the dead
ever wed,
share a bed?

Must forms old
repose cold
in the mold?

Decayed, homely,
their fate's only
to stay lonely?

Does love seep
to the deep
where they sleep?

Insensate,
must they wait
and not mate?

Or, beyond time,
will lay sublime
in beds of lime?

Styx

Christina Sng

The old bones
Snap in his jaws,
Spraying splinters
All over the floor.

I've taken a hair;
I've taken a tooth.
The tasty parts
I know he will choose.

I call down the gods
For justice and war
While my dog gnaws
On a broken femur.

They open the hellgates
To let out the beasts
As we patiently wait
Deep down in the crypt.

When the demons are done
And justice restored,
We return to the surface
To collect my reward.

No more long nights
Ferrying the dead,
No more dark days
Hiding their heads.

For once we can live
Free out of this cell,
Just me and my dog
By the gates of hell.

The Fairiest

Oliver Smith

The window was left unlatched in her room;
the curtains drawn, the bed still made, wooden
shutters flung aside, where down the ivy
she'd climbed: her shoes were lying in the leaves:
so we followed where her footprints danced

through roses wild, orchids pale, down the path
to the toadstool circles and blue-stone rings,
where fairies met for their midnight ball
and sang sweet changeling songs to call poor girls
from their dreams—to waltz in the glades of green.

We searched all through the wooded coomb:
in caves, in hollows, in burial ground;
in the boathouse where she used to hide;
but where we searched she could not be found,
though her dress lay folded by the riverside.

I hoped she danced, hand in hand, with fairer folk
in the gardens of another world, in lands
where woodbines lushly bloom; I hoped she slept
on a strong oak branch, under shining seas of stars
and the golden light of the harvest moon.

I dreamed she walked with me last night
along the track, her hand held tight in mine,
and where we went every plant was red in thorn
and green in claw, labyrinthine briars
uncoiled as she turned in the full moon's light.

And I saw her lying in a cold clay bed,
her body withered in spider web: bound
among hog-backed barrows and ancient vines
whose loom of roots in the damp and gloom
wove weft of bone with warp of tomb.

The Separation

Ian Futter

You bring my warm cadaver
to this place:
A living lie
from death's all-calming grace,
to show me how mere music
moves a beast,
and tell me how this corpse
can be released.

You grip my hand
and race me to the pit,
where bodies boil
amongst the sweat and spit.
That's where I lose you,
with the music; loud,
in heaving mass
transformed to concrete crowd.

This sweating swarm
which presses on my skin
knows not the monster
that they hold within,
and as I search the faces
for you, friend,
a halting heartbeat
stutters to its end.

If only with this dead eye
I could see
your blissful form—
that final part of me—
Then maybe I would not
feel time's harsh blade,
which hacks between
the maker and the made.

The Ghost Factory

F. J. Bergmann

The oldest stately homes are infested
with revenants—all those deaths
over centuries: poisoned husbands, stabbed
brides, inconvenient heirs and stepchildren,
guests lured into rooms whose doorways
were then bricked up.

Nouveaux riches find it easy
to arrange murders, on the premises
of their elegant townhouses and palatial
country estates or elsewhere, but ghosts
are anchored by family connections.
Even so, arrangements
can be made.

A bespoke ghost is tailored just for you—
and always meets your expectations.
We search out indigent relatives
you didn't know you had
or didn't care to know. In some cases,
if desired, we can . . . embind, shall we say,
black sheep, strayed daughters.

Naturally, you will want them installed
in a guest room, preferably in a separate
wing, preferably soundproofed.

Those guests who have experienced the . . .
experience we provide are quick
to spread the tale—instant cachet!

We specialize in stylish details,
touches that confer age and authenticity:
the dull glow of antique pearls; an almost-
imperceptible flutter, as of long eyelashes
or the heartbeat of a small brown bat;
the click of a trigger being pulled
halfway back over and over
inside a locked drawer.

We recommend that the room
contain neither windows nor mirrors
nor, indeed, anything reflective.
Let me also give you this card
for our exorcism specialist,
just in case.

The Baleful Beldam

Manuel Arenas

Around a toadstool fairy ring, ensconced in a darkened wood,
A bothy, blighted, lies where bides a crone who bodes no good.
Her garden bears a noisome bed of noxious flowerets;
Her hearth has been the mise-en-scène of hellish tête-à-têtes.
Her cauldron roils with viands queer, you would not care to eat.
Contrariwise, she feeds her imp with blood from out her teat.
Her ruddled eyeballs barely see, but she can sniff you out,
Then snatch you up in gnarly clutch to gut you like a trout.
Good many hapless mendicants have knocked upon her door,
Summarily ushered thither, then seen again no more.
Sometimes her shadow has been seen to dance in lunar light,
A-frolicking with woodland nymphs into the autumn night.
Upon the eve of All Saints' Day she flies astride her broom
And cackles as she casts a spell, with dolor fraught, and doom.

Remains

David C. Kopaska-Merkel

Among the ruins of the shattered lab,
A shadow moved or wisp of pale gray smoke,
The scent that lingers where foul garbage lay,
And something bitter burning in the throat.
No trace was found, no particle of bone,
The doc had left this world entire it seemed,
Yet after dark a phosphorescent glow
Would wax and wane and carmine motes would gleam.

At first the corpses in the ruin lay;
We found a desiccated shrew or cat,
Then in the lane and in the nearby fields
A cow, a horse, lay bubbling, charred, and flat.
This morning dead beside her car I found
My neighbor's severed head inside her hat.

Classic Reprints

Fright

May Sinclair

Fright.
I have been naughty to-day;
My mother sits in her chair,
With the dark of the room and the light
Of the fire on her face and hair.
Her head is turned away,
And she will not say
Good-night.
I kneel at her knees; I try
To touch her face; I throw
My body in torment down at her feet and cry
Quietly there in my fright.
For I think, perhaps, perhaps she will die in the night,
And never know
How sorry I am.
Surely, surely she will not let me go
Out of her sight,
Like this,
Without a word or a kiss?
I was her little lamb
Yesterday.

I climb the last stair
Where the gas burns always low.
In the big dark room my bed
Stands very small and white—

God—God—are You there?
I feel with my hands as I go;
The floor
Cries out under my tread;
Somebody shuts the door;
Somebody turns out the light
At the head of the stair;
And I know
That God isn't anywhere,
And that Mother will die in the night.

[From *Voices* 4, No. 3 (September 1920): 83–84.]

The Silent House

Samuel John Alexander

Knock! Knock! The door is barred.
Ye are true in watch and ward
Bolt and bar and lock, so witness these, my fingers, bruised and scarred.
Yet I know they would not feel
Though they beat on triple steel,
While I wrench the dreadful secret from its black and broken seal.

Oh, the dark, forbidding house
Frowns from black and angry brows,
Like a violated temple, brooding o'er its broken vows.
Surely, Something, silent shod,
In the middle night hath trod
In the inner holies, riving at the handiwork of God.

Speak! Speak! He will not speak
Though I cry out with a shriek;
Though the coward blood runs backward from the pallor of my cheek;
Though I cry out "It is I!"
Comes no answer to my cry
Save an echo, beaten backward from the adamantine sky.

Bring the axe and bring the bar;
Let us throw the door ajar
On the guilty Something, hiding where the trembling shadows are;
Something rending with its claw;
Dripping ravin from its jaw;

Springing up to tear asunder, crouching down again to gnaw.

    Nay, what ecstasy of fear.
    Nothing! There is nothing here
But the empty casket, rifled of the gem I held most dear.
    He hath gone, and gone with him
    Something vast and Something dim,
Something filling all the heavens to the far horizon's rim.

    Not as wild beasts tear their prey
    Death divorces soul from clay,
But he bears it on white wings above a flawed and futile day.
    Let us leave him with his light
    Bleakly, mystically white.
Let us wrap the shadows round us and go forth into the night.

[From Alexander's *The Inverted Torch and Other Poems* (San Francisco: A. M. Robertson, 1912).]

Articles

Clark Ashton Smith and Robert Nelson: Master and Apprentice (Part 3)

Marcos Legaria

Despite several acceptances by *Weird Tales* and the *Fantasy Fan*, Nelson found himself at a crossroads. Smith's reaction to "Under the Tomb"[1] was so tepid that Nelson turned his hand toward the short story:

> [. . .] As I said, I would use "Under the Tomb" as substance in a fantasy for TFF, which I have already written. I have also written a poem for TFF.[2] I have not sent either to you, because I want them to be a sort of 'surprise.' I do not care much for them anyway. But before I submit my first story to W.T. I should like to have you read it. However, I have not started one yet. But I shall let you know when I do. Well, I sent the two contributions to [editor Charles D.] Hornig, telling him he could have them to use in TFF or to burn in the furnace. And this is what he says: "I was indeed glad to receive your poem and story. The poem is very, very good, but the story, "The Last Feast" is *superb!* I personally believe that it is worthy of Lovecraft, (what about Nelson, Charles?) even if the horror is accentuated, (the substance from "Under the Tomb") I really mean that. But after all, I don't think the story would have been half as good if one horrific phrase was left out. I suppose you submitted it to Wright (I never did such a thing, Charles) and he rejected it on the grounds of too much horror. It is really new, as you say, and totally different

---

1. Nelson, letter to Smith (3 April 1934); ms., John Hay Library, Brown University (hereafter JHL).

2. "The Unremembered Realm," *Fantasy Fan* 1, No. 12 (August 1934): 188.

from any story I have ever seen before. In fact it is a lot better than half the stuff I've read in Weird Tales. (Thanks a lot Charles,—wait till you've seen my first story in Weird Tales. . . .) Of course, that's only my opinion, which isn't worth much I suppose, [. . .] but I know that it'll go over well in THE FANTASY FAN. I am so overstocked that it'll have to wait a few months, but I'll surely place it as soon as possible."[3]

Smith's well-intentioned guidance instead was a source of friction. Nelson had eagerly sent Smith "Sable Revery," "Dream-Stair," and "Under the Tomb," but when Smith pointed out their weaknesses, Nelson began to doubt the master.[4] The fantasy "The Last Feast" does not survive, and all we know of it is what Nelson and others relate in correspondence. Hornig noted that it was worthy of Lovecraft, but Nelson's additional correspondence to Smith describes his repentance in not showing the story to Smith first:

> I fear that I have unknowingly violated all of the ostensible good faith you have had in me. I should not have been so expeditious in sending my approximately-2959-word fantasy off to Hornig for use in The Fantasy Fan. The prime reason I did so was because I thought the tale would be labeled as "atrocious stuff" by anyone who read it. However, it is foolish: for you, of all persons, would surely give me your unbiased opinion. But Hornig read the story and thought it 'worthy of Lovecraft'! Now, of course, I do not believe it could be compared with Lovecraft in any way possible. I do not know; but, at any rate, I am writing Hornig, telling him to return the manuscript to me. Then I shall send it on to you via second-sheet form, the better to let me know if it could be made into something to submit to Weird Tales. It is not very long, and I do not believe it would bore you in anyway. It is something 'very different.' I believe. And I prefer to dub it: The Last Feast. It is a comedy–a comedy of tragic disenchantment.[5]

A month later, Nelson chronicles some of his own impressions of "The Last Feast," having absorbed some of Smith's reactions:

> And now, about my enclosed tale, "The Last Feast." First of all I want to say that I personally and truly do not care for it a whole lot. Yet, I think it has *some*

---

3. Nelson, letter to Smith (11 May 1934), quoting a letter to him from Hornig; ms., JHL.

4. Nelson, letter to Smith (8 March 1934); ms., JHL.

5. Nelson, letter to Smith (28 May 1934); ms., JHL.

potential qualities that could make it into something effective for Weird Tales. The chief objection, (which I think you will find and perhaps with some justification) is the "horrible" locution uttered by Exphele. And yet, Mr. Smith, it seems that I have successfully embodied this in an unprecedented and unique manner. Or perhaps I have not. I shall leave it to your better deduction. And the words said by Exphele, while being, perhaps, a bit unappealing, are, I do think, really nauseating and disgusting. However, let me know of this too.

Towards the end, when I say, "The prophecy had come true, if indeed it was a prophecy," I meant to infer, of course, that the catastrophe could very well have been a cataclysmic prank of Nature also; and at the same time I endeavored to 'do away' with the rather pasee architectural norm of the 'average' story-plot. All of the names, "Wharnside, Hawes, Brough, etc." are authentic, as the story is laid in England. And I have not, I hope, tricked the reader in any way. For illustration, instead of giving him the name of "Necronomicon" or some other spurious and wholly extinct volume, I give him Alexander Pope's "The Dunciad." However, the mention of Pope's volume has very little or no bearing upon the story at all. It was only a brought in as 'convincing atmosphere.'

"The Last Feast" was slow writing for me. Please know this to be true. It starts out rather slowly, but stay with it; there is more to come. On the whole, I think, you will agree that of all "different" stories, this story is most different: it has at least been my aim. The story slowly gathers momentum as it goes along and until to the very end. The ending I have strived to make unique, appealing, human, plausible. Do not be afraid to either condemn or praise my story. Either or both will be helpful for me. I perhaps should have left more space at the margins of the second-sheets for short jottings of criticism, etc. But I single-spaced and typed them in the manner I did, the better to avoid an over bulky envelope. There is enough postage on my self-addressed envelope, however, to ensure the story's return, besides a sheet or more, perhaps, of criticism.[6]

"The Last Feast" seemed promising, using Alexander Pope's The Dunciad rather than H. P. Lovecraft's Necronomicon, a fictitious tome alluded to by Lovecraft's devotees. On 28 June 1934, Nelson, with "The Last Feast" in hand, visited Wright on a busy day at the Weird Tales offices.[7] The previous day, Nelson and Hornig met in Chicago, but before this Nelson wrote to Smith what

---

6. Ibid.

7. Nelson, letter to Smith (6 July 1934); ms., JHL.

Hornig's thoughts of Nelson might be like: "I think he will be wondering what sort of a person *I* am, who writes such 'devastating' letters in T.F.F!!"[8] Nelson gives Smith a detailed description of his day after with Wright:

> [. . .] Then Wright recommended reading *The Last Feast* once more. In the revised version uttered by Exphele. These Wright liked very much. Fortunately, the tale required very little time in which to be read, and Wright finished with the reading of it [. . .]
>
> And this is Wright's verdict of *The Last Feast*: "It is a phantasmagoria-extravaganza, an extravaganza-phantasmagoria—there is no definite plot—then there is too much sex-interest—it becomes and is very interesting, but then you use some words which throw off the reader's reading balance—it is typed very neatly—there are no typographical errors—and the ending is just like Kent had woke up and found it was all a dream—the story would be all right for The Fantasy Fan—I think some day you will be writing for Weird Tales—"
>
> I said thanks and that someday I hoped I would be writing for Weird Tales.[9]

Shortly thereafter, Nelson wrote Wright his reasons for not wanting to resubmit "The Last Feast" to the *Fantasy Fan*. In Nelson's opinion, the story was foolish and its publication would detract from his reputation. He believed that weird literature should be serious in all aspects. In a letter lamenting Wright's rejection of the tale, Nelson outlines his philosophy of the true artist's place in his works:

> I am, of course, deeply grateful for your fine criticisms and suggestions regarding *The Last Feast*. And although I should have been happy had Wright accepted it, I now feel very happy that he did not. I have grown more and more to respect and appreciate his critiques. And I really think, (as I vaguely thought before) that The Last Feast is not really serious and convincing. And I think that all manner of fantastic literature really should be serious, the better for convincingness. And, at bottom, I am of a serious and melanchloly nature. I wish you to know this is true. And yet—going back to fantastic literature—humor may be taken for tragedy, and tragedy for humor. And the artist, whether he paints with his brush or with his pen, is never as a rule, able to clearly define his own individual creations as a student of

---

8. Nelson, letter to Smith (28 May 1934); ms., JHL.
9. Nelson, letter to Smith (6 July 1934); ms., JHL.

his work can: for the obscure explanations lie in the dark of his heart, in the depth of his mind.[10]

Smith's own tales of grim humor, such as "The Death of Malygris," and "The Charnel God," inspired Nelson.

Nelson soon sent Wright a poem with the two verses Wright approved of salvaged from "The Last Feast," with an additional stanza, and also the newly revised "Under the Tomb,"[11] vastly different from the version Nelson had sent Smith in May.[12] In June 1934, Nelson writes Smith that Wright accepted "Under the Tomb," but on the condition that some changes be made:

> Just received word from Wright on *Under the Tomb*. He likes the poem, and will take it; but not until 3 lines in it are changed somewhat. In the first stanza for example, the meter slips: "And like a strange flower grown from sable drugs." And the 3rd and 5th line in the second stanza sound somewhat forced he says: "Crones cankered suck and gnaw at witch-worms' fat." "And face of maid who bows sad violin." This after "While searing candles cleanse the rotting gloom" The poem just has 3 stanzas, as I mentioned in my last letter. The 3rd and last beginning, "Far still beneath, etc." as you probably remember. Ending in the last two lines, "There is an everlasting resonance [/] Pealed by the tomb in glad deliverance."[13]

Nelson's letters and poems have such a rebellious streak that he apologized to Smith for any misunderstandings he may have caused in their correspondence: "I know that you misinterpreted my last letter. You could not help but doing otherwise. Hereafter I shall and will master and predominate my prevailing spirits and emotions."[14] Nelson now was consumed by attempts at revision of his poem. He tells Smith: "I have gone over and over very carefully upon my poem, *Under the Tomb*. It has even caused me quite a number of sleepless but not visionless nights. This whole past week I have worked on three lines."[15] During this critical process, Nelson sent the poem a third time to Wright, apprising Smith of further changes. As has been demonstrated,

---

10. Nelson, letter to Smith (6 July 1934); ms., JHL.

11. Nelson, letter to Smith (6 July 1934); ms., JHL.

12. Nelson, letter to Smith (19 March 1934); ms., JHL.

13. Nelson, undated letter to Smith; ms., JHL.

14. Nelson, letter to Smith (14 July 1934); ms., JHL.

15. Ibid.

Nelson's poetic world has been charted with images and sounds mapping the genesis of "Under the Tomb," with the visitation of dreams impinging upon his compositions:

I have sent the revised poem to Wright, with high hopes that he will definitely accept it this time. That very bad line, 'crones cankered suck and gnaw at witch-worms' fat" I have changed entirely—and reads now: "The dead sup with the dead o'er flowing vat." This revised line is a part-affect of a horrible dream I had two nights ago. I should like to go into detail about the dream, but I fear it would be too distasteful and well displeasing to you. After the aforementioned revised line follows the present version of the last three lines of the second stanza:

"While searing candles cleanse the rotting gloom
And let young maid to her last tryst repair,
To die with maddened music and despair."[16]

These lines did not make it into the published version of the poem. The complete text of "Under the Tomb" can be presented here, as it appeared two months before Nelson's death in the May 1935 issue of *Weird Tales.*

Dread beings grope and sport in gory lakes,
A foul mist creeps and feeds on swollen slugs;
From beds of perfumed plants squirm fetid snakes,
And like a flower grown from sable drugs,
A moon of steel drips blood upon a sky
Darkened by what mad phantoms prophesy.

But this hath ceased and passed, and now in that
Mephitic, crumbling woodland 'neath the tomb
The dead sup with the dead o'er flowing vat
And searing candles cleanse the rotting gloom;
And they who stood in sorrow's joy and pain,
Tread now through hell's ecstatical refrain.

Far still beneath, where bloated babes are kept
In glacial rooms, and skulls are lit as lamps
To guide through the life beyond, and where are swept
Green veils of oozing slime and deadly damps,

---

16. Ibid.

> There is an everlasting resonance
> Pealed by the tomb in glad deliverance.

Relations between Nelson and Smith continued to be strained, as Nelson started noticing long delays in Smith's responses to his letters. Nelson was partly the cause of this, as he seemed to be alienating Smith in his letters. This was not a unique incident: friction with his parents has been mentioned, and it gradually spread to other loved ones and friends:

> I wish you would write to me sometime in the future. I no longer write to my cousin, (one less from my few dying-off correspondents list) for the absurd reason that he thinks his "girl friend" became enamored of me, while out on a trip here recently. The actual crux of the matter is this: she was forcing her attentions on me. Although she was pretty, I did not think her to be beautiful. And her views of things were certainly as silly and girlish as I have ever known. I am explaining all this in detail just as an instance in my fast-fallings friendships.

> Now there is only one friend who I see often in St. Charles, and he too is growing tired of me. I can only turn to one more: and he has been labeled as a Lesbian by many of our village guidance quidnuncs. [. . .] I have met and talked with him before. He is somewhat older than myself, a few years only, and he really is a charming fellow. I do not know what to do. If I renew my acquaintance with him people will begin to 'talk.' I think the best thing I can do is to remain alone.

> But all of this letter (I know) has been to no avail. And you will either laugh at it or scorn it or both. And I am sorry. Forgive me.[17]

Nelson was now becoming enamored of California poet George Sterling (1869–1926). Sterling himself had been mentor to Clark Ashton Smith when Smith was a teenager. When Nelson came across some of Smith's works in Wallace Alvin Briggs's *Great Poems of the English Language*—the collection noted by Wright to Smith—he also found the works by Sterling. Nelson relates this epiphany to Smith: "Poems of George Sterling were included. And these, I am sorry to say, are the only poems by Sterling that I have read. I hope that in the future I may be able to secure and read his entire works. I wonder if he had ever entertained thoughts of his suicide while he wrote *The Last Days*."[18] With Smith's assistance, Nelson wrote to Harry Robertson of San Francisco, son of

---

17. Ibid.

18. Nelson, letter to Smith (3 April 1934); ms., JHL.

A. M. Robertson, the publisher of Smith's first book, *The Star-Treader and Other Poems*, and of most of Sterling's books, inquiring as to their availability:

> I hope [. . .] to get Sterling's "The Wine of Wizardry." This is out of print. But he [Robertson] has a few left at $2.50. "Lilith" is $1.50. "Yosemite" is $1.00. "Beyond the Breakers," "Testimony of the Suns," and "Selected Poems" are out of print. But it is his intention to reprint these.
>
> He gave me two beautiful Sterling cards, "with his compliments," as he said. One, "The Cool, Gray City of Love," the other, "The City by the Sea." Both are really beautiful. The former I especially liked.
>
> To many minds, it would seem almost inconceivable why Sterling should have died by his own hand, for he seems, in such poems as the aforementioned two and the only other ones I have read: "Mirage," "The Lost Nymph," "The Master-Mariner," "Spring in Carmel," "The Last Days":
>
> > "Days departing linger and sigh;
> > Stars come soon to the quiet sky;
> > Buried voices, intimate, strange,
> > Cry to body and soul of Change;
> > Beauty, eternal fugitive,
> > Seeks the home that we cannot give."
>
> It seems to me that Sterling was for ever seeking that Beauty. Life, perhaps could not give it to him—not even his own poetry had still to find that beauty. And so he sought it in Death.[19]

One wonders what Smith thought when he read Nelson's reflections on the passing of his own mentor.

Despite tension between Smith and Nelson, Nelson remained a staunch defender of Smith. Forrest J Ackerman instigated "A Quarrel with Clark Ashton Smith" in a new column in *Fantasy Fan* called "The Boiling Point." Ackerman was irked that *Wonder Stories* published Smith's interplanetary horror tale "The Dweller in Martian Depths," a story he said belonged in *Weird Tales* instead. Correspondents and friends such as R. H. Barlow, August Derleth, and H. P. Lovecraft defended Smith and his story. They noted that the deficiencies in the tale were not Smith's fault, but the result of sloppy editorial tampering. One of Smith's chief advocates during this debate was none other than Robert Nelson.

---

19. Nelson, letter to Smith (5 June 1934); ms., JHL.

Nelson first wrote his defense of Smith to "The Boiling Point" in the November 1933 issue of the *Fantasy Fan*:

> The Ackerman–Smith controversy assumes all the aspects of a mad comedy. To assail and reprehend the writings of Clark Ashton Smith is as preposterous and futile as a dwarf transporting a huge mountain peak upon the tip of his tiny finger. Either Forrest J. Ackerman is daft or an imbecile or a notoriety-seeking clown or knave. Clark Ashton Smith stands alone in the realm of present-day weird and fantastic literature, and, therefore, above all his contemporaries. He is still King: and has yet to be dethroned.[20]

Nelson defended Smith once more in what would be the last installment of "The Boiling Point":

> When you shout, pertaining to Smith stories, 'May the ink dry up in the pen from which they flow!' you affect the refined and sensitive minds of the admirers of beautiful things, and cause them to exclaim, 'Here, indeed, is one who endeavors to do something in words as terrible as in actuality: cleave the head of a genius in twain!' Hence our fitting denunciation of you, Mr. Ackerman for attempting to backbite one of the greatest writers America has ever produced.[21]

Smith wrote Nelson his thoughts about the bad blood resulting from the "Boiling Point" imbroglio. Nelson reassures Smith that he remains a true artist, no matter what the cost:

> You should have no cause to feel sorry, Mr. Smith, if the recent argument in The Boiling Point of TFF aroused any ill-feeling. It *has*, Mr. Smith, and deservedly.
>
> It is tragic enough that you have been and are *still*, not appreciated nearly as you ought to be—but when this senseless bombastic, and damnable fool, Forrest J. Ackerman, comes along with his ax to attack you then it is a *noble* reason, Mr. Smith, that we who admire you above all others, come to your assistance.
>
> All that I wrote against Ackerman I shall never regret having written. And everything that I did write was entirely unfeigned, and above all, ingenious.[22]

Nelson's praise of Smith's work was genuine, as seen in another letter: "Your drawing for 'The Colossus of Ylourgne' is certainly in my opinion, the

---

20. *Fantasy Fan* 1, No. 3 (November 1933): 40.

21. *Fantasy Fan* 1, No. 5 (February 1934): 93.

22. Nelson, letter to Smith (16 April 1934); ms., JHL.

best drawing you have had so far, and is one of the weirdest of any *drawings* I have seen. And the story is one of the greatest I have ever read, to come from your pen or from the pen of anyone else!"[23]

Smith rewarded Nelson's praise of "The Colossus of Ylourgne" with the original artwork. "And many, many thanks for your drawing. I have it on my escritoire before me and I really find it difficult to remove the picture from my line of vision: it is convincingly *real.*"[24] This and other tales by Smith received an extra dose of commentary from Nelson:

> And once more let me say that I prefer to think of "The Colossus of Ylourgne" as the best tale by you that has appeared thus far in Weird Tales, [. . .] But perhaps you have had a greater story before this in W.T. of which I am not aware. And I have nearly forgotten to give some words of praise for "The Demon of the Flower," which appeared in the Dec. 1933 issue of Astounding Stories. [. . . L]et me know if you have any stories or poems appearing or that are scheduled to appear in any of the science fiction periodicals or other publications. I am subscribing to Marvel Tales and know you have a tale, "The White Sybil," scheduled. But are there any other publications besides M.T. and W.T. in which you are appearing? I should most certainly like to read them.[25]

After Nelson's July 1934 letter, no more correspondence was exchanged for a short time. The next month, Smith's mother accidentally scalded her foot, so Smith's household duties multiplied. A note finally arrived from Nelson with a photo of himself, with the envelope postmarked 14 November 1934: "The enclosed photo-snapshot of myself taken very recently, though of inferior finish and quality, will perhaps give you a good suggestion of my likeness."[26] The photo most likely was the one he sent Lovecraft at the time, who shared it with some of his correspondents.

Nelson's worsening relationship with his parents forced him to move out for a short time before returning home for the Christmas holiday. His fondness for Sterling's poetry helped him during this trying phase:

---

23. Nelson, letter to Smith (28 May 1934); ms., JHL.

24. Nelson, letter to Smith (5 June 1934); ms., JHL.

25. Nelson, letter to Smith (16 April 1934); ms., JHL.

26. Nelson, note to Smith [postmarked 14 November 1934]; ms., JHL.

I am back in St. Charles and have reached a happy reconciliation with my parents. My father, as well as my mother, admit and realize that they were not as sympathetic towards me as they should have been. I, in turn, when I learned this, felt sorry that I had left them.

Henceforth, I shall strive to follow the cure of George Sterling, in his poem, *The Balance*, in which he stresses, "Let us be fair"—"let us be fair"—Perhaps, after all, there are two sides to everything. Perhaps both I and my parents have made mistakes.

And so I have taken a new lease on life. And I have put all thoughts of despair and failure into the futile grave of yesterday's memory. And I think I have set my feet upon the garden of sun and hope, closing the dark gate behind me, and seeing a light which I knew existed but never saw till now.[27]

Nelson began to write his "Lost Excerpts" in the latter half of 1934. He probably did not show the prose poems to Smith in advance of their appearance in Hornig's *Fantasy Fan* and Donald A. Wollheim's *Phantagraph*. Nothing further is heard between Nelson and Smith in 1935.[28] Smith's mother passed away in May 1935, and Nelson himself died on 22 July, the eve of his birthday. Nelson's work under the guidance of Smith has been discussed in this essay, but one final major piece Smith read and gave his suggestions to was most likely sent by Nelson's parents to Wright. It is the epic poem "Jorgas." This last collaboration between the master and his apprentice appeared posthumously in the February 1936 issue of *Weird Tales*. In this poem Nelson ingeniously salvaged most of the lines omitted from "Dream-Stair."

> With sighs the potioned flowers stooped to kiss
> Pale Jorgas just awaking from his dream
> Of olent wine and swirling-shadowed bliss,
> And as the blue mist crawled upon the blade

---

27. Nelson, letter to Smith (21 December 1934); ms., JHL.

28. It should be noted that some of Smith's correspondence perished in a cabin fire. Another possibility related to the gap in the correspondence file is that after Smith's passing, Smith's widow Carol Smith gave or sold some of this material to bookdealer Roy A. Squires. Hence the Nelson–Smith file may not be complete. Oddly, H. P. Lovecraft and Clark Ashton Smith did not mention Nelson in their own correspondence. Perhaps Smith's letters to Nelson may one day emerge and shed more light on their unique working relationship.

The flowers talked and sang to him, and swayed
In shades with his, but all at once did scream,
"O Jorgas, why art thou a saddened man?"
"My thoughts are wildly blown with lunar dust,
My lips, wine-steeped, are sore from evil prongs,
I cannot break the thousand dream-wrought thongs
That trammel me with dreadful death and must."
"O Jorgas, wine...perfumes...no courtesan?..."
"Oh, cease, and leave me to my misery.
What poisoned hand is this that smooths a face
Of bronze and plucks thy bitter petals free?"
"O Jorgas, wine and shadows all embrace
Themselves with us and thee in ecstasy."
"No! no! I see...I hear...my eyes...that glare..."
"Pale one, look up...Her palm...Her heart...laid bare...
Take it, and she an orb will give to thee..."
"No! no! it is accurst! I know...I know
The vipers three who kissed and nuzzled it..."
"You dream as One who dreams below the Pit."
"I would let the flames to wrestle with the snow—"
"No, stay—take thou this knife and cut in twain
The throat of Him who offered thee domain
Within the realm where Specters laugh and dwell."
"Oh, do not say—what is there I can gain?
No! no! I would rather dream in silent hell . . ."
"He tramps on skulls and gluts on matted hair.
He comes—the Thing, whose noisome cerements shed,
Reveal the storm, the dead, in tortured tread.
O Jorgas, fare thee well! We die in prayer."
"Jorgas, I am He who comes in burning sod."
"My mind betrayed! Oh, do not slay me now!
Remove thy long-dead face and burnt-off brow—"
"Jorgas! Beat thy evil breast and cry for God!"

Reviews

A Guidebook for Witches and Warlocks

Donald Sidney-Fryer

FRANK COFFMAN. *The Coven's Hornbook and Other Poems: Weird, Horrific, Supernatural, Fantastic, Science Fictional, Broadly Speculative, and Traditional.* Preface by Donald Sidney-Fryer. Foreword by Frederick J. Mayer. Illustrations by Yves Tourigny. Bold Venture Press, 2019. 254 pp. $14.95 tpb.

This volume has fifteen separate sections, as well as a Glossary of Forms and an Alphabetical Index of Titles. The section titles are as evocative as the well-honed verses of the poems themselves. Let us list them:

Witchcraft and Warlockry
Ghosts and Hauntings
Sorcery and Summonings
The Lycanthropicon: Werewolves and Their Ilk
Lovecraftiana
Halloween/Samhain: A Chronographia of All Saints Eve
Vampires: The Undead
Ghoulies, Beasties, and Things that Go Bump in the Night
Arch Weirdness: The Inexplicable and Abnatural
Horribilis Mundus: Physical Fear and "the Mundanely Gruesome"
Fantasy and Myth: The Realms of Gold
Ekphrasis and Hommage: Poems on the Other Arts and for Some of my
Fellow Poets
Other Genres of the Imagination
Novus Ars Poetica and Wyrdskaldskaparmal

Metapoesis: Poetry about Poetry
Some Traditional Verses

This amazing "handbook"—a kind of collected (but not complete collected) poems—announces a major voice (in a single published volume) in American poetry of the fantastic and supernatural. The voice belongs to Frank Coffman, or (in full) Dean Franklin Coffman II.

I say forthrightly that this is one humdinger of a book. Although I would not suggest that you read it all at once from cover to cover—as I have only now done, rather at a gallop, in one fell swoop, even if over a period of days—I can certainly recommend that you somehow acquire a copy. It is a delectation of a poetic feast. Frank Coffman must rank as one of the most erudite poets whose work we have ever encountered so far. He is not just a master craftsman, above all as a sonneteer, and of the sonnet form in its innumerable variations (and there are many); he is also a master of many little-known metres, often of recondite provenance. What is more, he demonstrates mastery of them all, whether sonnets or metres or other forms.

It is best to read such a book as this by dipping into it here and there (perhaps one whole section per sitting) from time to time, and savoring several items on occasion. Do not do as I have done, rushing through the book from one end to the other. That procedure might turn out as exhilarating but also (alas!) exhausting. Do not imitate our example, a flagrant one of poor reading practice, especially of poetry.

I claim a certain fraternity with Coffman because he is not only a traditionalist as a poet but a damn good one. I have never presented myself as anything other than a traditionalist, thanks to the "ensample" of Edmund Spenser and his idiosyncratic forms and practices. I say this even if I admire good or great non-traditional poetry as much as the practitioners of it admire it themselves. Hence, as traditionalists, the bond of fraternity between Coffman and myself! We traditionalists must stand together, to counteract the disdain toward the traditionalists sometimes emanating from the non-traditionalists!

Proceeding from front to back, let me quote in whole or in part certain poems by a fellow practitioner that have struck and captured my fancy. Professor Coffman proffers a great many adventures to the lover of traditional poetry not just in arch-imaginative endeavor but in language and linguistics as well.

But before engaging with the main text, the "Dear Reader" should read, nay, *must* read the professor's introduction (a solid piece of work at five full pages). In this he lays out his credentials as a traditional, but innovative, Formalist practitioner, yes, of poetic forms and norms. For people no longer accustomed to reading poetry in formalist verse (particularly aloud) it is essential reading. For those acclimatized in traditional versification, even those readers might discover some surprises. As Clark Ashton Smith has observed, the forms and themes of poetry do not become outmoded or exhausted. The exhaustion inheres in the poets themselves. The good professor certainly demonstrates that the older forms and themes (that is, of love and fear) have not exhausted themselves.

As we proceed into the first poems presented here, we come up against a real problem: which poems to cite in whole or in part. Coffman has much to say, to relate, to narrate, but his uniformity of craft, with everything well honed, makes it almost impossible to choose which poems to highlight by quoting them. I might refer the reader, if of Keltic derivation, to the sections listed at the head of this review. The poems in "Witches and Warlocks," for example, abound in Keltic lore of all types, which the poet beautifully defines: Beltane, Lughnasadh, and Samhain, and so forth similarly.

One thing the reader gains is an admonition: treat older people with respect and circumspection, especially older women. Some "old crone" might turn into a sorceress, a necromancer, of great power. Show respect: dire things might otherwise occur!

To keep this notice within reasonable bounds, I shall quote only a handful or less of poems, among Coffman's unique shape-shifting art. But first and foremost, we cite in full the poet's own adumbrated poetic credo in "Prelude." It also serves as a fine example of a villanelle.

> Prelude
>
> They wind through Realms where what is "Real" is gone,
> These verses meant to urge the chill of Fear,
> These lines I've penned to show a different Zone.
>
> Perhaps best not read when you are alone,
> Some outline shapes—we hope *not really* here!
> Seeking Lost Lands whereof the "Real" is none.
>
> These visions, ragged, rough, I've sought to hone:
> Fantastic Worlds that sharpened from the blear.
> These scrawls outline a wholly different Zone.

They ring quite loud, or muffle with odd tone,
Born from the Dreams and Nightmares of a Seer
Who's traveled where no stuff of "Real" is known.

Turning this leaf, your Journey has begun.
This page is but a gateway! You are near!—
Traveler, most welcome to this different Zone.

Open the gate! There is much to be shown.
Look! Up ahead! Now hazy, but soon clear!—
Strange Visions never met, Weird Places never gone.
Come, Reader, and explore this different Zone.

Again, it is near impossible to give in this limited space any coherent idea of the wealth and variety in this collection of the author-poet's power of invention and imagination. A strong narrative drive manifests itself in virtually every morceau. These poems are much more than mere celebrations of isolated or static images. Coffman pays notable tribute to fellow poets, whether traditional or not. What might appear at first as mere cleverness usually leads to some deep and often ominous discovery.

Not all the selections are grim and ghastly. Several purposely fabricated "for Sir Arthur Conan Doyle" possess much urbanity and charm. The following may serve as an apt example.

The Repetitious Client

Many's the time I've climbed these stairs before
(I know the count: precisely seventeen);
Paused but a moment, knocked, then welcomed in
Where two friends wait, beyond that magic door.
I scan the room for old, familiar things:
The mail jack-knifed in mantelpiece is seen,
Cigars coal-scuttled, Persian slipper pouch,
Papers in disarray upon the couch.
The bullet pocks that praise Victoria, Queen.

I'm greeted warmly, asked to come along.
"The game's afoot!" you see, and we must go—
"No time to lose!" And once again I know
A case awaits us. And I hear the song

That beckons! And whither we shall see.
Adventure calls again to them—and me.

The poems commenting on other poems and poets appear particularly well done and memorable. Ditto for "an irregular Italian sonnet" evidently commenting on himself, the author-poet. We cannot resist quoting it in full.

Meta-Poesis

> I, meta-man, who searches his own soul
> And hyper-pens on keyboard ultra-thought,
> Who hopes in his faux-quilling, will be caught
> Some bits of mega-Truths as seasons roll.
> Such meta-tedium will take its toll:
> To contemplate the difficulties fraught
> With not-so-micro-dangers as we plot
> The demi-lines that sum some hoped-for whole.
>
> This meta-man too often semi-seeks
> To peek behind the ink upon the page.
> Why not just let each sentence max-engage
> The proto-reader? Hope some meaning leaks
> Through letters in this daring alpha-Bet?
> Send forth the veri-thing without regret.

Ending our notice, we can do no better than to quote in full the good professor's final selection, his profoundly manifested and embraced belief in poetry, and almost in the fervent sense of religion.

Credo

> Sweet summer solstice sun sets my blood surging;
> Wild winter blizzards blast my bleaching bones;
> The dew of the new dawn down is my sweat urging
> Damp of the dusk that seeps deep under stones,
> Cleansing the old roots and the new seeds purging.
>
> Bright burning leaves in autumn's ancient hues,
> Fall as do all that hopeful poets pen,
> Blown by the Winds of Time, waste and confuse
> Themselves in heaps. Most single leaves unseen—Then

To return to Earth, leaving behind no clues.

But starting buds of so-sweet greeny spring
Will come again after the Winter's blight.
Some herded words might be heard—That's the thing
That keeps the poet's quill aflight at night,
Hoping that some will savor, clutch, and cling.

Praying that some might hear and sing along
To the tune, in tune with Nature's native verse;
Touch some things human; delay—for brief or long—
The prancing worms that haul the poet's hearse:
For it is my fierce need to sing that song.

We should add that the art chosen for the cover is intriguing, and that for the frontispiece is gruesome and repulsive. In addition, the collection boasts six adroit and artful illustrations by Messire Yves Tourigny, seemingly perceived "Through a Glass Darkly."

Notes on Contributors

Manuel Arenas currently resides in Phoenix, Arizona, where he writes his Gothic fantasies and dark ditties sheltered behind heavy curtains, as he shuns the oppressive orb that glares down on him from the cloudless, dust filled desert sky. His work has appeared in various genre publications, most notably in the poetry journal *Spectral Realms.*

Chelsea Arrington has a predilection for things dark and romantic. Among her favorite authors are Algernon Charles Swinburne, Lord Dunsany, and Ray Bradbury. She likes her steaks rare and her wine as dry as graveyard dirt. Her poetry has appeared in the anthology *Folk Horror Revival: Corpse Roads*, *Spectral Realms*, and *The Audient Void*. She lives in Southern California with her boyfriend, her nephew, and two lap dogs.

Ross Balcom lives in Southern California. His poems have appeared in *Beyond Centauri*, *inkscrawl*, *Poetry Midwest*, *Scifaikuest*, *Star*Line*, and other publications. He is a frequent contributor to *Songs of Eretz Poetry Review.*

David Barker's latest books are *Witches in Dreamland*, a Lovecraftian novel written in collaboration with W. H. Pugmire, from Hippocampus Press, and *Half in Light, Half in Shadow*, a chapbook of weird short stories from Audient Void Publishing.

F. J. Bergmann edits poetry for *Mobius: The Journal of Social Change* and imagines tragedies on or near exoplanets. His work appears irregularly in *Analog*, *Asimov's*, *Polu Texni*, *Pulp Literature*, *Silver Blade*, and elsewhere. *A Catalogue of the Further Suns*, a collection of dystopian first-contact poems, won the 2017 Gold Line Press poetry chapbook contest and is available at fibitz.com.

Adam Bolivar, a native of Boston now residing in Portland, Oregon, published his weird fiction and poetry in the pages of *Nameless*, the *Lovecraft eZine*, *Spectral Realms*, and Chaosium's *Steampunk Cthulhu* and *Atomic Age Cthulhu* anthologies. His latest collection, *The Lay of Old Hex*, was published in 2017 by Hippocampus Press.

G. Sutton Breiding has been publishing poetry since the early 1970s. Among his poetry collections are *Autumn Roses* (1984), *Necklace of Blood* (1988), and *Journal of an Astronaut* (1992). He lives and works in West Virginia. A volume of his collected weird verse is in preparation.

Pat Calhoun works from an old house in Santa Rosa, California, that he shares with his wife, three cats, and a large collection of fantasy books. He wrote a column, "Weird Words," about vintage fantasy comics, that ran for fifteen years in Comic Book Marketplace and currently writes for the International Netsuke Society Journal. He is also busy editing *Weird and Wondrous: An Anthology of Fantasy Poems*, and writing a few of them as well.

G. O. Clark's writing has been published in *Asimov's, Analog, Daily SF, HWA Poetry Showcase*, and many other venues. He is the author of fourteen poetry collections (the most recent is *The Comfort of Screams*) and two fiction collections, including *Twists & Turns*, published in 2016. He has been a Bram Stoker Award finalist and was an Asimov's Readers' Award winner in 2001. He lives in Davis, Calif., in a mobile home entertained by books, CDs, streaming TV, and fading dreams.

Frank Coffman is a retired professor of college English and creative writing. He has published speculative poetry, fiction, and scholarly essays in a variety of magazines and anthologies. His poetic magnum opus, *The Coven's Hornbook and Other Poems* (January 2019), has been followed by his rendition into English verse of 327 quatrains in his collection *Khayyám's Rubáiyát* (May 2019). Both books were published by Bold Venture Press.

Christopher Collingwood was born and raised in Sydney, Australia. He graduated with a degree in business studies. He has devoted his spare time to writing, with works published in *Outposts of Beyond, Illumen, Neo-Opsis, Not One of Us, Empty Silos* (Inwood Indiana Book), *Fantastical Savannahs and Jungles* (Rogue Planet), and various works as part of the Oz Poetic Society.

Scott J. Couturier is a writer of the weird, grotesque, perverse, and darkly fantastic. His poetry and prose began appearing in journals and anthologies in 2017. Venues he has contributed to include the *Audient Void, Spectral Realms, Hinnom Magazine, Eternal Haunted Summer*, and *Weirdbook* (forthcoming). His fiction has been repeatedly featured in the *Test Patterns & Pulps* anthologies from Planet X Publications.

Ashley Dioses is a writer of dark poetry and fiction from southern California. Her debut collection of dark traditional poetry, *Diary of a Sorceress*, was released in 2017 from Hippocampus Press. Her second poetry collection of early works, *The Withering*, is forthcoming from Gehenna and Hinnom Books this autumn.

Ian Futter began writing stories and poems in his childhood, but only lately has started to share them. One of his poems appears in *The Darke Phantastique* (Cycatrix Press, 2014), and he continues to produce dark fiction for admirers of the surreal.

Liam Garriock is an author, prose-poet, and aspiring polymath who lives in Edinburgh, Scotland, or, alternatively, in a metaphysical borderland between "Aubrey Beardsley's ideally grotesque world" and Joseph Cornell's nostalgic dreamland. He likes to remain elusive.

Wade German is the author of *Dreams from a Black Nebula* (Hippocampus Press, 2014). His poetry has been nominated for the Pushcart, Rhysling, and Elgin Awards, and has received numerous honorable mentions in Ellen Datlow's *Best Horror of the Year* anthologies.

Maxwell Gold is an author of weird fiction and dark fantasy. His work has been published in *Spectral Realms*, *The Audient Void*, *Hinnom Magazine*, and elsewhere. His short story "A Credible Fear" will be published in the literary journal *The Offbeat* from Michigan State University's Department of Creative Writing and Rhetoric. He studied philosophy and political science at the University of Toledo and is an active member of the Horror Writers Association.

Norbert Góra is a poet and writer from Poland. Many of his horror, science fiction, and romance short stories have been published in his home country. He is also the author of many poems in English-language poetry anthologies around the world.

Cecelia Hopkins-Drewer lives in Adelaide, South Australia. She has had science fiction poetry published in the *Mentor*, a fanzine edited by Ron Clarke, and participates in an online poetry community known as "Poetry Soup." She also has flash fiction pieces in an anthology entitled *Worlds: Dark Drabbles #1*, edited by Dean Kershaw, and articles in the *Lovecraft Annual*. (She has also been known by her maiden name "Hopkins" and her married name "Drewer.")

Ron L. Johnson II has had photography published in *Photographer Forum Magazine* and has been published in the *St. Charles Suburban Journal*. Since digitalization has put film on the endangered list, he writes now with words instead of light. His writings are influenced by science, art, fantasy, and the macabre. If he talked to you, he wouldn't stop, and his grandma nicknamed him Ronnie Radio. However, now, his poems and stories do the talking.

David C. Kopaska-Merkel edited *Star*line* in the late 1990s and later served as president of the Science Fiction Poetry Association. His poetry has been published in scores of venues, including *Asimov's*, *Strange Horizons*, *Polu Texni*, and *Night Cry*. Kopaska-Merkel edits and publishes *Dreams and Nightmares*, a poetry zine in its thirty-third year of publication.

Geoffrey A. Landis is a science fiction writer and scientist. He has won the Hugo and Nebula awards for science fiction and is the author of the novel *Mars Crossing* and the story collection *Impact Parameter (and Other Quantum Realities)*. In his spare time, he goes to fencing tournaments so he can stab perfect strangers with a sword.

Randall D. Larson has been writing Lovecraftian and Bloch-ian fiction and nonfiction since the 1970s (*Eldritch Tales*, *The Arkham Sampler*, *Crypt of Cthulhu*, *Weird Worlds*, *Inhuman*, etc.) and has contributed to a number of books on weird fiction criticism. The bulk of his writing has been in the realm of film and film music commentary.

Curtis M. Lawson is the author of unapologetically weird and transgressive fiction, dark poetry, and graphic novels. His work ranges from technicolor pulp adventures to bleak cosmic horror and includes *the Devoured*, *It's a Bad, Bad, Bad, Bad World*, and *Black Pantheons*. He is a member of the Horror Writers Association and the organizer of the *Weird Live Horror* reading series. He lives in Salem, Mass., with his wife and their son.

Marcos Legaria is a scholar on H. P. Lovecraft, R. H. Barlow, Clark Ashton Smith, and related writers. His articles have appeared in the *Lovecraft Annual* and elsewhere.

Kurt Newton is a short story writer and novelist, but his first love is, and always will be, poetry. Over the last twenty years his poetry has appeared in a wide variety of magazines and anthologies including *Dreams and Nightmares*, *Star*Line*, *Mythic Delirium*, *Polu Texni*, *Hinnom Magazine*, *Corpse Roads*, and *The Book of Night*.

K. A. Opperman is a poet with a predilection for the strange, the Gothic, and the grotesque, continuing the macabre and fantastical tradition of such luminaries as Poe, Clark Ashton Smith, and H. P. Lovecraft. His first verse collection, *The Crimson Tome*, was published by Hippocampus Press in 2015.

Manuel Pérez-Campos's poetry has appeared previously in *Spectral Realms* and *Weird Fiction Review*. A collection of his poetry in the key of the weird is in progress; so is a collection of ground-breaking essays on H. P. Lovecraft. He lives in Bayamón, Puerto Rico.

Carl E. Reed is currently employed as the showroom manager for a window, siding, and door company just outside Chicago. Former jobs include U.S. marine, long-haul trucker, improvisational actor, cab driver, security guard, bus driver, door-to-door encyclopedia salesman, construction worker, and art show MC. His poetry has been published in the *Iconoclast* and *Spectral Realms*; short stories in *Black Gate* and *newWitch* magazines.

Allan Rozinski is a writer of speculative fiction and poetry who has most recently had poetry either accepted or published in *HWA Poetry Showcase Volume V*, *Spectral Realms*, *Outposts of Beyond*, *Star*Line*, and *Weirdbook*. He can be found on Facebook and Twitter.

Ann K. Schwader lives and writes in Colorado. Her most recent collections are *Dark Energies* (P'rea Press, 2015) and *Twisted in Dream* (Hippocampus Press, 2011). Her *Wild Hunt of the Stars* (Sam's Dot, 2010) and *Dark Energies* were Bram Stoker Award finalists. In 2018, she received the Science Fiction & Fantasy Poetry Association's Grand Master award. She is also a two-time Rhysling Award winner (2010 and 2015) and was the Poet Laureate for NecronomiCon Providence 2015.

Darrell Schweitzer is a short story writer and novelist, and former coeditor of *Weird Tales*. He has published much humorous Lovecraftian verse (*Non Compost*

Mentis [Zadok Allen, 1993] et al.) and also has two serious poetry collections in print, *Groping toward the Light* (Wildside Press, 2000) and *Ghosts of Past and Future* (Wildside Press, 2008).

Donald Sidney-Fryer is the author of *Songs and Sonnets Atlantean* (Arkham House, 1971), *Emperor of Dreams: A Clark Ashton Smith Bibliography* (Donald M. Grant, 1978), *The Atlantis Fragments* (Hippocampus Press, 2009), and many other volumes. He has edited Smith's *Poems in Prose* (Arkham House, 1965) and written many books and articles on California poets. His autobiography *Hobgoblin Apollo* (2016) and two volumes of miscellany, *Aesthetics Ho!* (2017) and *West of Wherevermore* (2019) have been published by Hippocampus Press.

Claire Smith's work mainly explores other worlds: the mythological, fairy tale, the supernatural and more. Her poetry has appeared, most recently, in journals and anthologies including earlier issues of *Spectral Realms, Illumen, Eye to the Telescope,* and *Riddled with Arrows.* She holds an M.A. in English from the Open University. She lives in Gloucestershire, UK, with her husband, the writer Oliver Smith, and their very spoiled Tonkinese cat.

Oliver Smith is an artist and writer from Cheltenham, Gloucestershire, UK. His poetry has appeared in *Dreams & Nightmares, Eye to the Telescope, Illumen, Mirror Dance, Rivet, Spectral Realms, Star*Line,* and *Weirdbook.* His collection of stories, *Stars Beneath the Ships,* was published by Ex Occidente Press in 2017, and many of his previously anthologized stories and poems are collected in *Basilisk Soup and Other Fantasies.* Oliver is currently studying for a Ph.D. in Creative Writing.

Christina Sng is the Bram Stoker Award–winning author of *A Collection of Nightmares* (Raw Dog Screaming Press, 2017). Her poetry has appeared in numerous venues worldwide, including *Apex Magazine, Cricket, New Myths, Polu Texni,* and *Space and Time,* and received nominations in the Rhysling Awards, the Dwarf Stars, the Elgin Awards, and honorable mentions in *The Year's Best Fantasy and Horror* and *The Best Horror of the Year.*

Tatiana Strange is a Gothic musician from Berlin. She is the author of *The Heroes of Dark Legends* and *Death Immortal.* In addition to her literary works she has also released a poetry EP on Bandcamp under the moniker Brazen Bloodshed, by which she is more commonly known.

Thomas Tyrrell has a Ph.D. in English Literature from Cardiff University. He is a two-time winner of the Terry Hetherington poetry award, and his writing has appeared in *Picaroon, Amaryllis, Wales Arts Review, isacoustic, Lonesome October, The Road Less Travelled, Three Days from a Cauldron,* and *Words for the Wild.*

M. F. Webb's poetry has appeared in previous issues of *Spectral Realms,* and her fiction has been published in Latchkey Tales. She hails from a Victorian seaport town in Washington State, which luckily is not too much like Innsmouth.

Abigail Wildes is a Gothic poet and writer whose work has appeared in *Obscurum 2: The Death Issue* and *Merchants of Misery: Authors Against Addiction.* She is currently working on a collection of New Gothic Poetry and *The Sad Little Tales of Annabelle Lee.*

Mary Krawczak Wilson has written poetry, fiction, plays, articles, and essays. She was born in St. Paul, Minnesota, and moved to Seattle in 1991. Her most recent essay appeared in the *American Rationalist.*

www.ingramcontent.com/pod-product-compliance
Lightning Source LLC
Chambersburg PA
CBHW060804050426
42449CB00008B/1522